Prosperity Made Easy

3 Keys to Financial Freedom

by

Ashley Terradez

Tulsa, OK

19 18 17 16   10 9 8 7 6 5 4 3 2 1

Prosperity Made Easy
ISBN: 978-1-68031-098-6
Copyright © 2016 by Ashley Terradez

Published by Harrison House Publishers
Tulsa, Oklahoma

Dedication

I would like to dedicate this book to my amazing wife, Carlie, and my awesome three children Zachary, Joshua, and Hannah.

Carlie, you are the most amazing human being I have ever met. You have mirrored God's pure, unconditional love and acceptance to me ever since we met all those years ago. (If you have not yet had the privilege of meeting my wife, you can find a full description of her in Proverbs 31:10-31!) Carlie, you are truly a virtuous wife, thank you for being you!

> "He who finds a true wife finds a good thing and obtains favor from the Lord"
>
> Proverbs 18:22 AMP

Zachary, Joshua, and Hannah, I am so privileged and thankful to be your dad. You all love Jesus and love people in your own unique ways! You, along with Mum, have become my best friends in the world! I have four crazy friends that are adventurous for Jesus—how great is that!

> "Children are a gift from the Lord; they are a reward from Him. Children born to a young man….how joyful is (that) man!"
>
> Psalms 127:3-5 NLT

Acknowledgments

I would like to thank my family members: my wife Carlie, and my children Zachary, Joshua and Hannah; my parents, Daniel and Linda (whom I put through so much they should be sainted!); my sister and brother-inlaw, Emma and David, and my in-laws, Barrie and Carol. I am blessed to have such a great, godly family!

I would like to thank the following people, whom all have had a major, positive impact on my life:

John Maycock

Rev. Paul Hamilton

Rev. Wendell Parr

Pastor Greg Mohr

This list of amazing men of God have walked with me through trials and celebrated with me in victories. Thank you for taking a chance and believing in me. Sometimes it seemed you were the only ones who did! I'll be forever grateful, and I love you all!

Special Thanks:

Andrew Wommack – www.awmi.net Thank you for meeting with us on March 18, 2006, and turning our world right-side-up forever! It's an absolute privilege to serve at your ministry.

Pastor Lawson Perdue - www.charischristiancenter.com Thank you for being my pastor and for all your support and love—both practically and spiritually. You have helped me grow in so many ways.

Billy Epperhart - www.billyepperhart.com Thank you for your sponsorship of this book and for your wise counsel in my life. I greatly appreciate all you do for me.

Catalyst Media - www.creatingcatalyst.com Thank you for making this book a reality!

Pastor Ben Conway, Tree of Life Network - www. treeoflifechurch. org.uk and Thomas L Colter. Thank you for your donations towards this project.

Table of Contents

Foreword

Financial prosperity is one of the most controversial subjects in the body of Christ today. Paul said covetousness (lust for money and what it can buy) is idolatry (Colossians 3:5), and the love of money is the root of all evil (1 Timothy 6:10).

This has led many to take the stand that we shouldn't believe God for financial prosperity. That the Lord will somehow just make everything we really need come to us automatically. Some have even gone as far as to advocate poverty as being godly.

In this book, Ashley Terradez accurately shows that financial prosperity was purchased for us by Jesus. Religious attitudes against prosperity are some of the strongholds that limit God's supply to us, and Ashley challenges these wrong beliefs.

I've known Ashley and his family since the night in 2006 when God miraculously healed their daughter, Hannah, who was at the point of death. I've seen them take hold of the truths of God's Word as I wish everyone would. They are now impacting people world wide for God's kingdom.

One of the areas of God's Word that they have a God-given revelation on is finances. Ashley is a giver. He's a fanatical giver. It's hard to out give him. And I've seen him prosper far beyond just his paycheck. The Lord has become Ashley's source, and it shows.

This isn't something reserved just for Ashley. The Lord wants all of us to prosper and be in health. In this book, Ashley gives very practical steps of how you too can enter into God's abundance.

Getting money shouldn't be anyone's goal, but every godly goal takes money. Without it, goals are deferred or abandoned. Many Christians are deprived of the money they need to accomplish God's instructions because of wrong thinking about money. Ashley deals with many of religions wrong concepts about prosperity.

If you know the Lord has more prosperity for you than what you are experiencing, I believe this book is for you. Open your heart and mind as Ashley leads you on a journey that will take you to a new level of having your needs supernaturally met.

- Andrew Wommack

Author, president and founder of Andrew Wommack Ministries, Inc. and Charis Bible College.

www.awmi.com

Introduction

Years ago, as I sat reading a book, waiting for my plane to land, one of my traveling companions leaned over and asked, "What'cha reading, Ashley?" I showed him the book by a well-known Christian author, and he said, "Oh, finances. I thought it was something important."

His comment really bothered me and for the next several days, I thought about it often. *Why are finances considered unimportant? Everybody deals with them. Why doesn't the Church teach about true biblical prosperity? They're always asking for money. Why do Christians file finances under nonspiritual aspects of life?* As I kept mulling over those thoughts, I came to the conclusion that finances scare people—especially Christians.

Many Christians hold an unbiblical view of finances. Their ideas and expectations about money are often based on the world's system or unbalanced church doctrines, when they should be based on biblical principles. Jesus taught about finances more than any other subject. Why? Because heart issues are extremely important to God, and finances reflect what's happening in our hearts.

Ecclesiastes 10:19 says, "Money answers everything." It touches every aspect of our lives. Without money, we can't care for our families. We need money to buy food, clothes, housing, healthcare, and even education. Without money, ministries can't preach the gospel, feed the hungry, or help the orphaned. Yet Jesus called money "that which is least."

> He who is faithful in what is least is faithful also in much; and he who is unjust in what is least is unjust also in much. Therefore if you have not been faithful in the unrighteous mammon, who will commit to your trust the true riches?
>
> Luke 16:10-11

The way we deal with personal finances is the way we deal with other things in life. Money is a reflector. If we're stingy with our money, we'll be stingy with our time. If we aggressively seek money, we're likely aggressive in relationships. If we're late paying our bills, then we're probably late for work or meetings. The way we handle money reflects the issues of our heart and ultimately spills over into other areas of our lives.

A few years ago, I got my first dog. It was a cute little retriever, but I knew nothing about training dogs. I thought, *It'll be okay; it's just a puppy.* But my wife told me, "That puppy is going to grow up to be 100 pounds of guard dog! You'd better think about training it."

I understood what she meant a few weeks later. The pup had gotten ahold of some meat, but it was too much for him to eat. So I bent down to grab the extra and saved it for later. In that moment, my cute little puppy turned on me, and *GRAH!* He snapped. It was terrifying! Somehow my cute little pup had become a vicious monster in my eyes. How embarrassing to be scared of my own dog!

So I sought the advice of an expert. He said, "You've got to be the alpha dog. Dogs are designed to either lead or follow. There is no middle ground. You have to show him you're the leader."

It's the same with finances. Jesus put it this way: "You cannot serve both God and money" (Matthew 6:24). None of us intends to serve money, but money is often the determining factor in our decisions. One of the biggest characteristics in a servant-master relationship is the master's responsibility to tell the servant what to do. The master leads; the servant obeys.

How do you decide what to eat at a restaurant? Do you order what you're in the mood to eat or do you look at the menu and order based on price? How do you decide where to go on vacation, what car to buy, or how much to give in an offering? If your money (or lack of it) is the determining factor in these decisions, then your money is leading you.

Please understand, I am not talking about stewardship here. I'm talking about the heart issues many of us deal with when we talk about finances. Nothing else contends for our heart like finances. Jesus said, "Where your treasure is, there your heart will be also" (Matthew 6:21). Our hearts and our finances are connected. That's why it's so important we have the right relationship with finances and understand the biblical tripod of financial prosperity. We have to learn to lead our finances or our finances will lead us, and someone will get hurt!

Part One

Thorns

Behold, a sower went out to sow... And some seed fell among thorns; and the thorns grew up and choked it, and it yielded no crop. But other seed fell on good ground and yielded a crop that sprang up, increased and produced: some thirtyfold, some sixty, and some a hundred.

Mark 4:3, 7-8

Chapter One

Infidel Christianity

Salvation is an all-inclusive word. Its root word, *sozo*, means "to rescue," and refers to the way God rescues us from the destruction of sin and delivers us into His life (Strong's Concordance, s.v. "sozo"). But salvation doesn't stop there! The Greek word for salvation is *soteria*, which means more than safety. It includes wholeness and refers to both the physical and emotional aspects of our welfare—even our finances (Strong's Concordance, s.v. "soteria").

When Jesus delivered salvation in His death and resurrection, He exchanged His life with ours (2 Corinthians 5:21, 8:9; Isaiah 53:4-5) and provided for our entire wellbeing—spirit, soul, and body. Scripture says we are now, "more than conquerors" (Romans 8:37). What does it mean to be "more than a conqueror?"

Picture two boxers contending in a championship match. When the two heavyweights jump into the boxing ring, it's usually a pretty good fight. Before long the ring is full of blood, sweat, and tears; and ten rounds have passed. Eventually someone goes down for the count... ONE... TWO... THREE..., and the crowd hears, "Ladies and gentlemen, the Heavyweight Champion of the World!" Officials bring out a huge gold belt, raise the conqueror's arms, and give him his purse. Then his wife jumps the rope, kisses him, and takes his prize to the closest mall. He may have been the conqueror, but she was "more than a conqueror!"

Jesus conquered sin and death for us on the cross in the same manner. When we receive what His grace did by faith, we become "more than a conqueror." Like the boxer's wife, we get the benefits without the blood, sweat, and tears. So what are the benefits of our salvation? One of them is the promise of provision (Genesis 22:14, Psalm 34:9-10, Philippians 4:19, 2 Corinthians 9:8, Matthew 6:32-33).

People often misunderstand that word. According to Merriam-Webster, provision is "the act or process of supplying" and "what is done in advance to prepare for something else" (Merriam-Webster Online Dictionary, s.v. "provision"). Provision is the behind-the-scenes work that makes what is being provided possible. I once heard a minister say, "God is your provision, but He won't make your lunch." I love that. God is faithful to do His part (making your prosperity possible), but you must do your part and respond to His grace with active faith.

James tells us that active faith does something with what it believes (James 2:17, 26). If we believe that God is our provision — that He will "supply all our needs" (Philippians 4:19) so that we will "lack no good thing" (Psalm 34:9-10) as the Word declares — then we will trust Him with our giving (2 Corinthians 9:7), steward what He provides (Acts 17:25), and live as an example to unbelievers in our work, speech, and attitude (Titus 3:14, 1 Timothy 4:12).

Unfortunately, many Christians take a selfish or lazy stance on God's Word. They dissect it, taking verses out of context to fit within their doctrines of experience. Or they completely remove passages of the Word to create an inoffensive faith. But this nullifies God's Word (Mark 7:13), and creates a generation of immature believers who've never seen the benefits of their salvation. These people struggle through life hoping for better things in eternity, but not really making a difference today. Though I doubt they've intentionally done it, they've become "hearers of the Word" only. If we want to see the promises of God's Word fulfilled in our lives, we must be "doers of the Word" (James 1:22)—the whole Word of God.

Too often Christians try to disguise their laziness with spirituality. In the name of faith, I've seen men frustrate their children, embitter their wives, and slander their bosses. They use the Word of God to manipulate or excuse themselves from responsibility and become infidel Christians. In a letter to Timothy, Paul addressed this problem when he saw it creeping into the church. He said;

> But if anyone does not provide for his own, and especially for those of his household, he has denied the faith and is worse than an unbeliever.
>
> Timothy 5:8

The <u>King James</u> version says, "he is worse than an infidel." Those are fighting words where I come from! I wrestled with God about this. *How could You call a believer "worse than an infidel?"* But look how the Amplified version says it:

> If anyone fails to provide for his relatives, and especially for those of his own family, he has disowned the faith [by failing to accompany it with fruits] and is worse than an unbeliever [who performs his obligation in these matters].

The Lord showed me that an unbeliever doesn't believe in God. For them, there is no provider. They carry the sole responsibility for their family. They can't pass the buck like some out-of-balance believers do, thinking, *Well, God promised to provide*, while they sit around idle. An unbeliever does everything they can to provide for their families. They look at their kids and feel the burden of responsibly that says, "Either I go out and provide, or we go hungry." They have no faith. They can't afford to be lazy and believe for God's provision because they don't believe in God!

Unfortunately, many of us who do believe don't really understand faith. As discussed before, active faith includes the element of obedience — doing what the Word says. As Christians, we are often guilty of putting all responsibility on God saying, "Well God, You promised You're going to provide all my needs. You promised You're going to look after me. I'm Your child; You need to keep Your Word."

But God has already performed His Word. Do you remember the definition of provision — "what is done in advance to prepare"? God provided for us, in advance of our need, in the person of Jesus! He also gave us the power we need to become a "doer of the Word" (Philippians 2:13).

According to James, refusing to do what the Word says creates deception in ourselves (James 1:22). I've been there. At one time in my life, I remember God correcting me with the revelation that I was believing one of His promises but not doing what the Word said in order to receive it. I was expecting the promise to supernaturally fall in my lap. But that's not how God's promises work. They require active participation.

I once knew a man who found himself, like me, in a very dangerous place spiritually. He confessed the Word and believed that God would provide for his family, but he was an infidel Christian. I know that sounds harsh, but it's true. He was a "speaker" but not a "doer" of the Word. It got so bad, his family started living out of their car. They couldn't even stay in the same parking lot for more than a few nights at a time. He came to me and said, "I just don't understand why God isn't providing for us."

"Do you have a job?" I asked.

"No."

"Have you been looking for work?"

"No."

"What are you doing then?"

"I'm just waiting for God to provide," he responded.

It reminded me of the story about the guy caught in a flood. He climbed out on the roof of his house, and prayed for God to save him. Soon a boat came along, and the driver said, "Can I help?"

"No," the man replied, "God's going to save me." Then a rescue copter flew over. "We've come to save you," the pilot shouted. "I don't need your help. God's told me He's going to save me," the man shouted back.

Another boat approached the man, but he waved them off. Before long, the man grew tired and couldn't hold on to his roof any longer. He slid quietly into the water and drowned. In heaven, he asked God, "Why didn't You come? I thought You were going to save me."

God said, "I sent two boats and a helicopter..."

God is a supernatural God, but He works in natural ways. We need to be careful that we don't become so spiritual, so out-of-balance, that we miss what God is practically doing in our lives. Scripture tells us that God gives us the power to get wealth (Deuteronomy 8:18) and that His blessing is without sorrow (Proverbs 10:22). But it also says, "in all labor there is profit" (Proverbs 14:23).

Did you know that God gave Adam work in the Garden of Eden? Before sin, before the curse, "the LORD God took the man and put him in the garden of Eden to work it and take care of it" (Genesis 2:15, NIV). Work is a blessing from God. It wasn't until Adam and Eve chose to sin that work became toil and began producing thorns and thistles. Genesis 3 says;

> Then to Adam He said, "Because you have heeded the voice of your wife, and have eaten from the tree of which I commanded you, saying, 'You shall not eat of it': Cursed is the ground for your sake; in toil you shall eat of it all the days of your life. Both thorns and thistles it shall bring forth for you, and you shall eat the herb of the field. In the sweat of your face you shall eat bread till you return to the ground, for out of it you were taken; For dust you are, and to dust you shall return."
>
> Genesis 3:17-19

After Adam's sin, the land began bearing thorns and thistles. His work became hard and frustrating. He did the same amount of work, but now thorns hindered his progress, and he produced far less than before. No matter how hard he worked, he produced barely enough or not enough. And this trend of toil continued. Work was cursed. Haggai says;

> "You have sown much, and bring in little; you eat, but do not have enough; you drink, but you are not filled with drink; you clothe yourselves, but no one is warm; and he who earns wages, earns wages to put into a bag with holes"
>
> Haggai 1:6

But praise God, Jesus changed that! Galatians tells us that,

> Christ has redeemed us from the curse of the law, having become a curse for us (for it is written, "Cursed

is everyone who hangs on a tree"), that the blessing of Abraham might come upon the Gentiles in Christ Jesus, that we might receive the promise of the Spirit through faith.   Galatians 3:13-14

When the Roman soldiers made a crown of thorns and pushed it on Jesus' head, blood ran down His brow like the sweat of a man toiling in the fields (Matthew 27:29). At that moment, Jesus exchanged His toil for ours. Now we work "as unto the Lord" (Colossians 3:23), and God's favor makes our efforts successful (Psalm 90:17). We've been redeemed from unprofitable, frustrating work. We are no longer cursed with painful, never-quite-enough toil. The work of our hands are blessed (Deuteronomy 28:12). But if we don't put our hands to something, how can God bless them? Work is the natural thing God uses to supernaturally provide for our lives.

I work with a man who left his job in corporate America to help a ministry in Colorado Springs. When he first moved his family to Colorado, the ministry he came to help couldn't support him. They didn't have a position open or the means to open one for a guy they'd never met, so my coworker began volunteering. One day, while he was putting gas in his car, the Lord spoke to his heart. He had been asking God how to provide for his family yet still obey His instructions to help this ministry. The Lord told him, "There's work right in front of you."

At 7-11, *God? You're joking*, he thought. Even though he came from corporate America and felt 7-11 was well below his paygrade, he also knew he had heard from the Lord. So he did it. He was hired on at 7-11 to cover the night shift at the worst hourly rate possible. His main responsibility was cleaning the slushy machine, but he did it "as unto the Lord" (Colossians 3:23).

As this man continued to show up faithfully to work, he received promotion after promotion. Within three years, he became 7-11's regional manager with 50 stores under his supervision! With each promotion, his pay increased until he was making more than he'd left behind in corporate America. His willingness to work opened the door for God to bless and promote him, and eventually enabled him to quit 7-11 and work full-time at the ministry he'd come to Colorado to help.

Chapter Two

Analog Thinking in a Digital World

God wants each of us to experience His benefits. He doesn't want us suffering in lack. He created us to succeed and desires that we prosper (3 John 1:2 and Genesis 1:28). So why are so many people trapped in the cycles of debt and poverty? If God promised to provide for our needs (Philippians 4:19), why aren't needs being provided for?

Remember Jesus' parable of the sower? He said everything in the kingdom works by this principle of sowing and reaping (Matthew 13:11):

> A sower went out to sow. And it happened as he sowed, that some seed fell by the wayside; and the birds of the air came and devoured it. Some fell on stony ground, where it did not have much earth; and immediately it sprang up because it had no depth of earth. But when the sun was up it was scorched, and because it had no root it withered away. And some seed fell among thorns; and the thorns grew up and choked it, and it yielded no crop. But other seed feel on good group and yielded a crop

that sprang up, increased and produced: some thirtyfold, some sixty, and some a hundred.

Mark 4:3-8

When Jesus explained this parable to His disciples, He said the seed was the Word of God (or we could say God's promises). Like seed, God's Word is sown everywhere, but according to this parable, it produces differently in different conditions. Why? One reason is thorns.

> Now these are the ones sown among thorns; they are the ones who hear the word, and the cares of this world, the deceitfulness of riches, and the desire for other things entering in choke the word, and it becomes unfruitful.
>
> Mark 4:18-19

Some hearts have become so hardened to God's Word they completely reject seed. Others have not been cultivated for strong root systems. Still others produce thorns that choke God's Word. What amazes me is that most thorns grow out of an unbalanced relationship with money (the cares of this world, the deceitfulness of riches, and the lust for other things). Only a small percentage of hearts produce fruit like the Word—but what a return they give, "some thirty, some sixty, and some hundredfold what was sown" (Mark 3:8 NIV)!

Are thorns growing up in your financial belief system? Do you have an unbalanced view of prosperity, taking only part of the Word and leaving the rest? Are you being a "doer of the Word?" Have you allowed the world's definition of wealth to skew your own? In an attempt to avoid greed, have you forgotten "all His benefits?" I don't know about you, but I want God to receive a return on His investment in me. I want my life to produce a hundredfold return!

But how much control do I have over that return? Hopefully, by now you understand that God's promised benefits don't automatically happen in our lives. God provided for us in grace, but our faith must respond. God will never force His will or His plan on us. We must make a decision to cooperate with Him. We must prepare the soil of our hearts.

If you're reading this book, I'm assuming your heart doesn't fall into the hardened category. You haven't rejected God's Word, nor are you attempting to live in your own wisdom or by your own ingenuity. That means you must be cultivating or weeding the soil of your heart. Even those of us who have worked to develop good soil, must diligently keep it.

> Keep your heart with all diligence, for out of it spring the issues of life.
>
> Proverbs 4:23

So let's look at some of the thorns that may be growing up in our hearts and robbing us of our benefits in Christ. One of the thorns many of us need to examine is unbelief. As we discussed earlier, we must become a "doer of the Word" if we expect that Word to work in our lives. It's amazing how the things we truly believe naturally create corresponding action.

For example, several years ago, Colorado Springs dealt with some pretty severe wildfires. At that time, my family lived in an older area of town with lots of mature trees and bluffs. Even though we were in town, it was a very private area; we couldn't see our neighbors. Unfortunately, the lay of the land and heavy undergrowth made that area of town one of the hardest hit.

During this time, we got a lot of phone calls from concerned family and friends. At one point, I remember getting lots of text messages from people saying, "Hey, you need to leave now. The fire's coming your way."

"I understand," I said. "We're watching the news. But it's still miles away. We're fine."

One of our friends even said, "You don't believe you're in danger, do you?"

"I understand it's a dangerous situation, but everything's okay."

You see I didn't really believe the fire was coming my way; I thought the reports were exaggerated. *If it was really that bad, my neighbors would be leaving too*, I thought. I didn't realize it, but all my neighbors had left.

Eventually, I took one of my four-wheelers to the top of the bluff on our property. Looking out over the bluff, I saw a 50-foot flame of fire only a quarter mile away. Suddenly, I believed! I left the four-wheeler on the bluff and ran back to my house like my pants were already on fire. "Quick! Carlie! Kids! Get in the RV!"

Thankfully, we had everything already loaded in case we had to evacuate. All we needed were the pets. We loaded the dog, the rabbit, the guinea pigs, but where were the stupid cats? "There's no time," I shouted at my daughter. "Get in the RV!"

"But Dad," she said starting to cry, "they'll burn."

"That's alright," I said before caving. "Hang on. I'll go find them." When we finally got loaded, we drove to a friend's house and stayed with them until the danger passed. A week later, the fire was under control and we moved back into our house. (God truly blessed us. The fire had changed directions, and none of our property was damaged. Our house didn't even smell like smoke!) But what I truly believed produced a corresponding action that day. What you truly believe about God's Word will produce a corresponding action in your life.

Another thorn we've discussed is the relationship we have with money. Jesus said, "You cannot serve both God and money" (Matthew 6:24). And although no one purposefully seeks to serve money, we have all probably found ourselves allowing money to be our master in the decision-making process. Remember, masters call the shots and servants follow through.

I can be a sucker for this. Every time I go into a clothing store, my wife says, "You're like a moth drawn to light when it comes to clearance sections." I remember buying a pair of shoes once that really didn't fit. The original price was close to $150, but all my discounts brought them down to $30. Every time I wore those shoes, I thought about what a deal they'd been; until I started getting pains in my upper thigh. In that situation, finances told me what to wear.

We can't allow finances to be the biggest voice in our head. That warps our relationship with money and elevates it to master status. In Matthew, Jesus said that place of authority belongs only to God.

> But seek first the kingdom of God and His righteousness, and all these things shall be added to you.
>
> Matthew 6:33

This entire chapter in Matthew exhorts us to not worry about the things we're going to eat and drink and wear. Worry exalts. It brings trivial things to the forefront of our minds and subtly makes them idols. When we let money be the biggest voice in our head, we remove God from His rightful position. But God promised that if we keep Him first place, He'll make sure our trivial needs are met. I once heard a minister say, "Obey God, and leave the consequences to Him!"

Sometimes the thorns that creep into our hearts are less obvious. Sometimes the thorns that hinder us from experiencing financial provision come in the form of worldly viewpoints or wrong expectations. As humans, we have a God-given desire to succeed, which means we often do everything we can to avoid failure. We tend to limit what we can do with what we've already done or at least what we've seen done. "This is the way my father did it," we say, or, "I know this will work; I heard so-and-so did it," or "I've never seen anyone do that."

This type of thinking limits what we can experience of God's provision. It's based on the status quo. It doesn't consider God's Word or utilize the creativity—the ideas and dreams—He's given to each of us. I like to call it analog thinking in a digital world. Analog thinking works if you live in an analog world. But we don't. Our world has changed since our parents' and grandparents' time. It's even changed since last year!

We no longer live in the Agricultural Age when every person physically supplied food for his family and hoped to sell the excess to buy whatever else was needed. We no longer live in the Industrial Age when a person went to school, learned a skill, got a job, and retired at age 55 with a pension. We live in the Information Age, and this age requires different thinking.

I understand that trying to think in a new way is daunting. It goes against our desire to avoid failure. But I find the Information Age exciting! Everyone now has access to the same set of information. It doesn't matter if you're from America or Malawi. It doesn't matter if you were born in a wealthy family or on the "wrong side of the tracks." Your background no longer limits what you can and can't accomplish in life. The Internet created a level playing field. Concepts that used to cost thousands of dollars to learn are now available at the touch of a button. Business models that, in the past, took years of trial and error to prove are now accessible in a half hour. It's amazing!

You no longer have to go to school, learn a skill, and retire on that skill. If you've dreamed of opening a small business, you can go online, research appropriate business models, learn how to create a business plan, and register your new business in less than a day. With all that information, your chances of success are much greater than in previous generations.

Education is extremely important in any age, but in this age, we need to ensure we're being educated in the right things. For years, schools have tried to educate kids like they were still in the Industrial Age. At one point a few years ago, students were getting degrees in super-specialized areas of personal interest, but they were completely unprepared to market themselves in the workforce. (There are, of course, some jobs that require specialized degrees — and I'm glad they do. I'd hate to have to go to a doctor for legal advice. Neither would I want to fly across the Atlantic if a pilot's only education was in business accounting.) But there's no point getting a college degree in Klingon. Specialized degrees stand out, but not for marketability! Recently, schools have begun responding to this shift in thinking and have started adding entrepreneurial classes to their graduation requirements, even in elementary school, which I find exciting.

In order to prosper in this new age, we have to make ourselves desirable to an employer and do something that adds value to the marketplace. The good news is there are so many ways to do that now. We can be employed. We can be self-employed. We can own a business. We can invest. We can even do several things at once! I know many people who have full-time jobs and work a business in the evenings or on weekends. I know others who own their own businesses and use their profits to invest.

Opportunities abound. And the Bible declares that we have been given a great advantage!

> Who, then, are those who fear the LORD? He will instruct them in the ways they should choose. They will spend their days in prosperity, and their descendants will inherit the land. The LORD confides in those who fear him; he makes his covenant known to them.
>
> Psalm 25:12-14 NIV

The only limits on our potential are those we give ourselves. Just a couple hours a day can make a big difference. I know a man who owns an eBay store. Instead of playing video games to unwind and fill his quiet hours in the evenings, he works his store. The first year he made $5,000 in extra income. The next year it increased, and increased again. Soon he was making over $100,000 a year in his spare time. If he wanted, he could quit his job and easily live off his business income. (Though I think he has plans beyond mere survival!)

Carlie and I have used eBay many times to make extra money. When we lived in England, I actually used eBay to sell cars. But I remember one time when the kids were little, we found a great deal on a wooden train set they loved playing with. We accidently bought one they already had so Carlie put it on eBay. That train set was soon bid up to twice what we paid for it! Carlie went back to the store and bought five more. Over the course of the next week, they all sold. So she went back and bought every set she could get her hands on. She was listing them by the dozens! We've done that several times. Sometimes we find collector's items at yard sales or in thrift stores; we buy them and resell them on eBay or Craigslist. Thanks to the Internet and smart phones, our learning curve has shortened. Now we can look up an item before we buy it to make sure it will sell at a profit.

There are so many opportunities out there to make money or get out of debt. We just need the eyes to see them.

Do not despise these small beginnings, for the LORD rejoices to see the work begin.

Zechariah 4:10 NLT

It's okay to start small. Small things have the potential for growth. But you have to start somewhere. Only God can make something out of nothing! The first place everybody can start is to become employed. If you're employed, you get paid to make your boss money. The more money you make for him, the more you get paid. You could also be self-employed. If you're self-employed, customers pay you to solve their problems. The better you solve their problems, the more customers you get and the more money you make. But both of these types of income have limits.

There is only so much one person can do. In either of these positions, you'll eventually find yourself limited by time or education, by strength or resources. However, if you own a business, those limits expand. Now you're paying others to make you money, and regardless of your personal limits, you can draw on others' strengths. In a business, whether or not your expertise or presence is there, you make money. Even better, when you invest, your money makes money without your help.

It's interesting to me that nearly 90 percent of all Americans survive off employment or self-employment earnings, but roughly 90 percent of the money moving around our country goes to business owners and investors! That's why they say, "the rich get richer." The amount of money a business owner or investor can make is limitless. Because their profits cease being tied to what they can personally accomplish, it becomes about their system. Does the system work? Are they surrounded by people who know what they're doing? Are they marketing effectively? Can they streamline the system to boost profits? Is there another door of opportunity they've yet to open?

The amazing thing about the Information Age in which we live is that it doesn't take special education or skill to develop more than one stream of income. Each of us can keep the security of a full-time, employed position and grow a small business in our spare time. Each of us can get out of debt and put our extra income into investments that will make even more money with little effort on our part.

Obviously, none of this happens overnight, but if we learn to recognize our personal thorns and begin cultivating right thinking—thinking that considers God's Word above our circumstances—we will discover the opportunities God has surrounded us with. It will become easier to make money and therefore, it will be easier to give, not only our money but also our time. Ultimately, the building of our financial wealth is not about us. It's about establishing God's covenant.

> And you shall remember the LORD your God, for it is He who gives you power to get wealth, that He may establish His covenant which He swore to your fathers, as it is this day.
>
> Deuteronomy 8:18

Chapter Three

Making Money Work for You

Money is a tool. Alone, it holds no power for good or evil. Can money do good? Absolutely. Has it been used for evil? Of course. But people's heart attitudes are what drive money's accomplishments.

If I took a Ben Franklin to Mexico, it wouldn't do me any good until I exchanged it for pesos. Again, if someone gave me a hundred Cambodian riels, I could do nothing with them in the US until I traded them for our currency. (I still couldn't do much with 100 riels—that's less than one penny!) The point is, money itself is irrelevant. Instead of focusing on money (and getting more of it), we need to focus on what money can do in the hands of people whose heart attitudes match God's.

My dad used to repair cars. He was a body man. In his day, the most important tool he owned was a hammer. Whenever a car was damaged, his job was to beat and mold its panels back into shape with his collection of hammers. When I was a little kid, I found one of the hammers he had just finished cleaning and polishing. It was so perfect; it screamed out to me to use it.

So I did. I took his hammer and started beating all the rocks I could find. I even split a couple! But my dad wasn't as thrilled with my accomplishment as I was. He was very generous with me, but I learned the value of good tools that day.

No matter what your trade, you value the tools needed for it. A teacher values her education; without it, she couldn't get a job. A chef values his cookware because without it, he's limited to the type of food he can make. A cabbie values his car. A doctor values his medicines. Every professional values their tools the same way my dad valued his hammers—not for what they were, but for what he could accomplish with them. We should value money the same way. Money is a tool, and in the right hands, it can accomplish amazing things for God's kingdom.

So how do we make money work for us? In the parable of the talents, Jesus answered that question:

> For the kingdom of heaven is like a man traveling to a far country, who called his own servants and delivered his goods to them. And to one he gave five talents, to another two, and to another one, to each according to his own ability; and immediately he went on a journey. Then he who had received the five talents went and traded with them, and made another five talents. And likewise he who had received two gained two more also. But he who had received one went and dug in the ground, and hid his lord's money.
>
> Matthew 25:14-18

I used to think this story was a little harsh, a bit biased. *The master must like that guy better to give him more than the rest,* I thought, but then I realized it said he gave to them "according to their ability." These were the master's servants. He had a relationship with each of them. He'd watched their work habits and ethics for years and knew what each one could handle. He entrusted money to them "according to their ability."

Notice how the servant with five talents and the servant with two talents each doubled their money. How did they do that? The scripture says they "went and traded." Maybe one of them kept running his master's business. Maybe one bought some tools and hired himself out as a laborer. Maybe they bought and sold merchandise. Maybe they invested in someone else's venture. Maybe they lost money, and then made more. All we know is they "went."

Unlike the lazy servant, the two good servants did something with what they were given. Neither sat around hoping their talent would split at the atomic level and miraculously create more of itself; they put it to work. Even the servant with only two talents did everything he could to give his master a return on his investment. He didn't complain about the difference in the initial distribution of talents. He didn't say, "That's not fair. He got more than me. There's no way I can make a go at this with only two talents." He put his money to work.

No matter what situation you find yourself in, use what's in your hand and put it to work. It will take diligence, but it will also bring great reward! For example, my daughter wanted to start a dog walking business. She did some research and decided the best way to use her time was to walk more than one dog at once. She found a coupler leash that would let her walk up to four dogs at a time. It cost $11. Hannah didn't have $11, so she came to me looking for an investor, "Dad, can I have $11?"

"You can make $11," I told her. "Figure out how you can make $11."

One day when I came home from work, Hannah handed me $11 when I walked through the door. "Would you please get on Amazon and buy me that leash? Here's my $11," she said.

"How'd you get that?" I asked.

Apparently she'd found an organic dog treat recipe online and used the flour and eggs we had in the pantry to bake them. She packaged them up in Ziploc bags, printed out a little flyer of the ingredients with an advertisement for her business, and stapled it to the bag. She then went around our neighborhood and sold each bag for a dollar. Hannah used what she had and got her leash! (I'm still thinking about how she should repay that non-affirmed initial investment from my pantry!)

Opportunities surround us; we just need the right attitude to see them. Whether we provide a service or sell goods, we must remember it is God who gives us the power to gain wealth so we can establish His covenant (Deuteronomy 8:18). The more money we make, the more money we can give. It may sound selfish, but if the motive behind our desire for money is giving, then God will give us the opportunities to make it.

> Now may He who supplies seed to the sower, and bread
> for food, supply and multiply the seed you have sown
> and increase the fruits of your righteousness.
>
> 2 Corinthians 9:10

People often make the mistake of thinking they have to do something completely new to make money. They read stories of multi-millionaires creating a new product or developing a new software and overlook what's already in their hand. They think, *I can't do that* or *I don't have those kinds of skills*, and miss the opportunities God has put in front of them. What are you good at right now? What do you already know how to do? What skills or interests do you have? What is your passion? Look around you right now. The things you see are what God will use to increase and prosper you. You just need to realize that they can be opportunities.

Find something you're interested in, research it, and ask God to give you creative ideas for making that hobby into a money-making venture. Brainstorm with me for a minute. Divide a piece of paper into fourths and label each fourth "hobbies," "previous employment," "skills," and "me." Then in each section, record three to five different skills, hobbies, or work experiences you have; be creative. In the "me" section, describe yourself (especially relationally or in regards to previous commitments). Your paper might look like this:

Hobbies	Previous Employment
Watching movies	Preschool Teacher
Gardening	Retail Sales Manager
Riding motorcycles	Merchandising
Decorating	
Skills	All About Me
Organizing	Married, mother of 3
Painting and crafts	Stay-at-home mom
Good memory	Volunteers at kids' school
Explaining things	Lives in city

Using the information in our example, we can create a list of jobs and/or businesses this person is already qualified for or (with a little research) might be interested in pursuing. Taking into account her previous commitments, she would likely prefer the flexible scheduling of self-employment. Her background as a retail sales manager tells me she ought to understand customer service, pricing, and marketing strategies, which will help her sell her own products. She enjoys gardening, but lives in the city (which means people have less space for gardening). She could develop a business around container gardening or another specialty area like xeriscaping. As a stay-at-home mom, she probably doesn't have the funds or space to buy, store, and sell the actual plants, so she could develop garden plans for different size gardens or areas of the country. By including extras (like pictures of what the finished garden will look like, care instructions, recommended nurseries, and suggestions for substitute plants) and offering these items for immediate download, she adds value to her product and oversells the competition. By using the Internet for selling (on either her own website or a site like Etsy), she will have almost no overhead and will open up her customer base to anyone with access to a computer.

The possibilities are endless. Maybe instead of sales, she wants to offer a service. With her interests and skills, she could become a professional organizer. The thing with services, though, is that you often have to have referrals to generate more clients. So how do you create referrals with no clients? You offer your services for free.

She could talk to her friends and ask to help them organize part of their house. She could take before and after pictures, and ask her friends to write up a testimonial or referral for her services. Something like, "Since my friend organized my kitchen, it's cut my prep time by 30 percent. Even my husband commented on how much easier it is to find things in the pantry. She was a god-send." Now she can advertise! She could make some business cards, put out an ad on Craigslist, and ask her other friends to help spread the word.

But what if I lose money? That's called an education. Now you know what not to do next time. Some of the most common mistakes people in services make is miscalculating their time and underbidding projects, but that's an easy fix. Simply increase your bid next time you work on a similar project. In sales, people often don't make the profit margins they anticipate because they don't market correctly. Maybe they bought something with only a seasonal market and took a loss. Next time, they'll know to hold the snow blower they picked up last summer and sell at the right time—after the first big snow.

Be diligent. Not everything's going to be an instant success. Some things won't succeed at all, but at the very least, you'll learn. Sir James Dyson (the developer of Dyson vacuums) went through 5,126 failed prototypes before finding one that worked. Now he's worth nearly $4.5 billion! Unfortunately, he went through his entire life savings and had to find investors before discovering the one idea that worked. We don't want to do that; that's why I counsel people to start businesses that require little to no initial investment. Then if it doesn't work, their savings are still intact, and they've not endangered their family.

The most important thing you can to do to ensure success is to not give up at the first hint of challenge. Mistakes can be a great learning platform. Learn, research, and try again. Keep a journal. Record what you've tried, what worked, what didn't, why you think it didn't, and what you'd like to try differently. Make money work for you.

The plans of the diligent lead to profit as surely as haste leads to poverty.

Proverbs 21:5 NIV

By making a plan for our money and investing in what we already know how to do (or already have interest in), we can make money work for us instead of always working for money. When our kids were little, we bought a diesel RV at an auction in England. As soon as they gave us the keys, we climbed into inspect it and thank God for His blessing. "Thank You Jesus for this RV," we prayed. "This vehicle will provide us with some good, memorable vacations and let us visit and minster to people." As soon as we said "amen," the kids were running around, turning nobs, pushing buttons, and opening cupboards. One of the cupboards they opened was hiding a half-dozen balloons that said, "Happy Birthday Jesus!" It was fun watching the kids squeal at that surprise.

We ended up taking that RV on a 4,000-mile road trip around Europe. We spent about a month visiting family, enjoying good restaurants and beaches, and touring France and Spain while the kids were out of school. We had a great family vacation, and at the end of the summer, sold the RV and nearly doubled our money on it. Its selling price even paid for our entire vacation!

"I can't do that," you say. "I don't know anything about buying and selling cars." You're right, you may not have the knowledge it takes to do exactly what I do with vehicles. But I bet you can do something. You have to discover what it is that God has placed in *your* hands and use that to create another stream of income for you and your family to prosper (Ecclesiastes 11:2).

God doesn't need our money, but He does need us to prosper. Without prosperity (having more than enough), we can't "give unto every good work" and be a part of establishing God's covenant on the earth (2 Corinthians 9:8). We need to prosper God's way so the message of the Gospel can be preached to all the world (Matthew 24:14). The Gospel may be free, but the road it travels is expensive!

Part Two

Barns

Honor the LORD with your possessions, and with the firstfruits of all your increase; So your barns will be filled with plenty, and your vats will overflow with new wine.

Proverbs 3:9-10

Chapter Four

Faithful with the Least

Financial prosperity has as much or more to do with the way we spend money than with the way we make it. No matter how much (or little) money we make, learning to properly manage it is vital to experiencing prosperity. It amazes me how many people think financial freedom is all about making more money. Making money is important—we've already discussed that—but how you manage money once it's in your hand is more important.

I know many people who have good jobs, make a good income, but do not manage what they have and struggle through day-to-day life. They always worry about how they're going to pay their bills. Their family spends little quality time together (because Mom and Dad are always trying to earn more money), and they complain about not having extra to give. But I know others who make a fraction of what they make, yet manage money well, and always seem to get ahead. You see, what we make is not as important as what we do with what we make. Even if someone makes $200,000 per year, spending $201,000 per year will ensure they never experience prosperity.

If we continue reading in Matthew about Jesus' parable of the talents, we'll see this principle of stewardship at work:

> After a long time the lord of those servants came and settled accounts with them. So he who had received five talents came and brought five other talents, saying, "Lord, you delivered to me five talents; look, I have gained five more talents besides them." His lord said to him, "Well done, good and faithful servant; you were faithful over a few things, I will make you ruler over many things. Enter into the joy of your lord." He also who had received two talents came and said, "Lord, you delivered to me two talents; look, I have gained two more talents besides them." His lord said to him, "Well done, good and faithful servant; you have been faithful over a few things, I will make you ruler over many things. Enter into the joy of your lord." Then he who had received the one talent came and said, "Lord, I knew you to be a hard man, reaping where you have not sown, and gathering where you have not scattered seed. And I was afraid, and went and hid your talent in the ground. Look, there you have what is yours." But his lord answered and said to him, "You wicked and lazy servant, you knew that I reap where I have not sown, and gather where I have not scattered seed. So you ought to have deposited my money with the bankers, and at my coming I would have received back my own with interest. Therefore take the talent from him, and give it to him who has ten talents."
>
> Matthew 25:19-28

Faithful with the Least

Notice how the servant with five talents and the servant with two talents received the same reward, even though they brought their master different amounts. The important thing wasn't how many talents each had, but what they had done with what they had.

Just like the men in this parable, we may not be responsible for what we're given in life, but we are responsible for what we do with what we're given. After my wife and I got married, we decided that no matter how much money we made, we wouldn't go into consumer debt. Even though my first position as a youth pastor came with a very small income, we decided not to use credit cards and spend money we didn't have. I remember going into the supermarket early in our marriage and thinking, *I've only got enough money to buy coffee or cereal. Would I rather be hungry and not tired, or tired and not hungry?* It was a tough decision, and it wasn't the only tough decision we had to make. But because Carlie and I learned to manage our finances and were diligent to live within our means, the little we started with began to grow. Soon we could walk into the supermarket and buy both cereal and coffee.

Now at the time, no one would have looked at Carlie and me and said, "Wow, look at them prosper!" But we were prospering. You see, prosperity is a process; it doesn't happen overnight. Genesis says:

Then Isaac sowed in that land, and reaped in the same

year a hundredfold; and the LORD blessed him. The man began to prosper, and continued prospering until he became very prosperous.

Genesis 26:12-13 (emphasis added)

Prosperity starts with right attitudes about money; it builds on the principles of stewardship in God's Word, and culminates with the ability to give. Now when Carlie and I walk into a supermarket, we can buy someone else's cereal and coffee! Why? Because we learned that true, biblical prosperity is not about how much you have, it's about how much you can give.

We often get this backwards—especially in the west. When I wholesaled cars back in England, I used to visit a place regularly without getting much attention. Then one week, I drove up in a convertible I was selling. It was a real nice Lotus Elise. The paint finish on that car was perfect; the engine purred. It was a beautiful car. As I was getting out, the owner of the place saw me, jumped up, and opened the door for me. I thought, *I've been here every week for months, and no one has ever treated me like I was somebody special—until now.*

This happens all the time. As human beings, we have the tendency to look at outward appearances (1 Samuel 16:7). We look at what someone has, where they live, how they're dressed, or what they drive and make judgments about them personally. But according to Jesus, biblical prosperity has nothing to do with our possessions.

And He said to them, "Take heed and beware of covetousness, for one's life does not consist in the abundance of the things he possesses."

Luke 12:15

Most of us in the developed Western world have more than enough "stuff." Some of us have so much stuff we pay other people to take care of it. We're very spoiled here. I say spoiled instead of blessed because of what we do with our abundance. The majority of the world lives in houses the size of some of our garages. They count themselves blessed to have food on the table and two chairs to sit upon, because now they have something to share with others.

You've heard it before, but it bears repeating. In Genesis, God told Abraham, 'I will bless you and make your name great. And you shall be a blessing" (Genesis 12:2). God didn't bless Abraham just so he could bless others, but because he was blessed, Abraham did bless those around him. The same is true of us.

Let me explain. If the only reason God blesses us financially is so that we can be a blessing, that would be like me giving my oldest son a new bike for Christmas so he could give it away. He would get excited, grab that bike, and run towards the door until I said, "Hang on, son. That's not really for you. I'm only giving that to you so you can give it to your younger brother." It's ridiculous, but that's what a lot of Christians believe.

The truth is, giving is a natural byproduct of God's blessing in our life. God doesn't save us just so we can offer salvation to others; He saves us because He loves us. God doesn't heal us just so we can be a testimony of His power; He heals us because He loves us. Do we tell others about our experiences with salvation and healing? Sure we do, but that sharing is a byproduct; it comes from a natural overflow of thankfulness. Prosperity is the same. God blesses us because He loves us, and that blessing should produce the natural overflow of giving. But if we don't manage our money properly, we will have nothing to give.

Ephesians 4:28 says, "Let him who stole steal no longer, but rather let him labor, working with his hands what is good, that he may have something to give him who has need." I was on an airplane once, flying without Carlie and the kids, when I noticed a man across the aisle from me. During our long flight, his hands were full of two little ones crying out in hunger. I saw him pull out the in-flight menu, glance at the high prices, and turn to his kids and say, "We'll just have to wait till we get to the airport." Like all kids, they weren't satisfied with that. "I'm hungry, Daddy. I'm hungry," they kept saying.

I felt the Lord nudge me to buy them lunch. It didn't make a lot of sense. The man looked like he had the money to take care of lunch; he just didn't want to spend it on an overpriced airplane sandwich (not that I blame him). But I wanted to obey the Lord, so I introduced myself and asked if I could buy him and his family lunch.

"Oh, no. That's not necessary," he said.

"I really want to," I replied. "I don't have my kids with me today, and it would make me happy to buy them lunch."

"Well, if you insist," he said.

So I bought them lunch. When we landed, I noticed his arms overflowing with baggage and babies, so I helped him again and carried his bag. Soon we were talking. He found out I worked at a Bible school, and all the way through the airport and while we waited at the baggage claim, we talked. He asked all kinds of questions about the Lord and the Bible. I got to sow the seeds of the gospel in his heart.

Remember the old saying, "People don't care how much you know until they know how much you care"? It's true. Because I was generous with that man, he opened the door of his heart to the love of God.

People are important to God. We are His greatest commodity. Jesus said, in Luke 16,

> He who is faithful in what is least is faithful also in much; and he who is unjust in what is least is unjust also in much. Therefore if you have not been faithful in the unrighteous mammon, who will commit to your trust the true riches? Luke 16:10-11

In these verses, Jesus says that our attitude towards money reflects our heart's attitude towards the true riches of God—people. These verses in Luke fall at the end of one of Jesus' parables about financial stewardship (Luke 16:1-13). Throughout the parable, He compares the world's shrewd use of money with the believer's unwise use. In verse 9, He says, ["Use worldly wealth to gain friends"] (NIV). *Why would He say that? That's what the heathen do!* That was Jesus' point. Heathens are shrewd with their money; they use it to promote their own interests and welfare. But often, as Christians, we misuse finances and ignore their use in promoting God's interest and the welfare of others. We need to learn how to be "faithful with the least," stewarding our money with godly principals so we have enough to give and God can establish His covenant in the earth (2 Corinthians 9:8 and Deuteronomy 8:18).

One of the most basic (and overlooked) financial stewardship principles is planning. Proverbs says, "A wicked man puts up a bold front, but an upright man gives thought to his ways" (Proverbs 21:29 NIV). Do you know where your money is going? Have you given thought to its ways and created a financial plan? Have you listed out your goals? Habakkuk 2:2 says, "Write the vision and make it plain on tablets, that he may run who reads it."

It's amazing what happens when you start taking control of your finances. Creating a written plan subtly boosts your level of financial accountability. It encourages you to be diligent so you can see your goals fulfilled. And diligence opens the door to supernatural blessing.

He who has a slack hand becomes poor, but the hand of the diligent makes rich.

Proverbs 10:4

Faithful with the Least

The soul of a lazy man desires, and has nothing; but the soul of the diligent shall be made rich.

Proverbs 13:4

The plans of the diligent lead surely to plenty, but those of everyone who is hasty, surely to poverty.

Proverbs 21:5

Although finances are "the least of things," they are important. The proper use of our finances helps God to establish His covenant. And when God prospers us, the scripture says there is "no sorrow with it" (Proverbs 10:22). Prospering God's way doesn't require huge sacrifices. There's no need to sacrifice family time, marriage, or health. All we need to do is obey.

If you are willing and obedient, you shall eat the good of the land.

Isaiah 1:19

Chapter Five

The Income Gap

The process of stewardship, "the conducting, supervising, or managing of something; especially the careful and responsible management of something entrusted to one's care," includes creating a written plan (Merriam-Webster Online Dictionary, s.v. "stewardship"). Some people call this budgeting. I like to call it setting priorities.

To me, the term "priorities" looks at the spirit of a thing. Instead of seeing a list of dos and don'ts and feeling guilty for spending money in one category over another, setting priorities makes me consider the long-term financial consequences of my decisions. My first priority (no matter how much money comes in) is always God (Matthew 6:33). Giving honors God. It is a tangible act of faith that says, "I trust You, God. I recognize that You have given me the power to gain this wealth, and it is You who can multiply it to meet my needs."

Honor the LORD with your possessions, and with the firstfruits of all your increase; so your barns will be filled with plenty, and your vats will overflow with new wine.

Proverbs 3:9-10

My second priority is me. That may be surprising, but I've found that if I don't pay myself, then I don't get paid. "That sounds awfully selfish," you say. "What do you mean pay yourself?" I mean saving or investing. If saving money doesn't become a priority, it will never happen. You will never have enough and will always feel that what you do have dwindles too quickly. Believe it or not, saving is a biblical principal.

Proverbs 11:24 says, "there's one who withholds more than is right." So apparently, we can withhold what is right. Withholding (saving) what is right would be saving for emergencies or for large purchases or to give. Saving out of a love for money or a trust in riches makes us like the man in Jesus' parable in Luke 12. One year, this rich man produced a great harvest, but instead of using that harvest appropriately, he decided to build a bigger barn to house it all. He thought, *All I have to do is save this and be set for life! I can "eat, drink, and be merry" without thought to anything else.* The rich man put his trust in riches, but it was misplaced, and his life was taken. Jesus said, "This is how it will be with anyone who stores up things for himself but is not rich toward God" (Luke 12:16-21 NIV).

Saving (with the right attitude) is like an insurance policy. It won't make you rich, but it will stop you from being poor. There's power in saving. Deuteronomy 28 says that God blesses the storehouse of the believer (Deuteronomy 28:8), but you have to have a storehouse in order for it to be blessed! At the very least, you need some sort of emergency fund that will help you survive life's unexpected storms. Too many people live paycheck to paycheck; then when the car needs new tires or someone has to see a doctor, they feel the full force of life's storm. Depending on the extent of their emergency, that thunderstorm can feel like a hurricane. But having savings creates a cushion between you and life; it knocks that hurricane-feeling back to a thunderstorm warning (Ecclesiastes 10:19).

One of the easiest ways to start paying yourself is to have a small percentage of your paycheck automatically deposited into a separate bank account. As long as the account is free, you'll not miss the $20 to $50 taken out, but you will notice the $500-$1000 saved in a year's time! You can invest the same way.

I would suggest using a separate account for your saving or investing than your checking account, so that money can't easily be transferred from one to the other. Also consider setting up the account with no checks or debit or credit cards attached. That way it's more difficult to get to your money, and that protects your savings from the latest gadget or new designer outfit. An account like this requires you to physically go to the bank for withdrawls, which lessens the likelihood of impulse purchases.

My next priority is always bills. You've got to pay your bills. When you sign a mortgage contract or open a utilities account, you essentially make an oath to repay someone. And oaths are serious business.

> [He] who keeps his oath even when it hurts…will never
> be shaken.
>
> Psalm 15:4-5 NIV

As a Christian, the way we give our word, make a promise, or sign a contract advertises God's character. That is not something to be taken lightly. Failing to keep our word paints an incorrect picture of God. We're told to,

> Let your light so shine before men, that they may see your
> good works and glorify your Father in heaven.
>
> Matthew 5:16

Borrowing money (which we'll talk more in depth about later) creates stress. Proverbs says, "The rich rule over the poor, and the borrower is servant to the lender" (Proverbs 22:7). Who wants to be a servant their entire life? Servanthood is hard. It doesn't come naturally. God created us to have dominion (Genesis 1:28) over life—not people. But it's hard to do that when we make ourselves financial servants. I had a friend who bought a bunch of real estate in 2006. He started renting out the houses he bought, leveraging the equity, and remortgaging them for extra cash. Soon he owed 110-120% on each house.

Everything was going fine, and he felt on top of the world until the banks called his notes. "You've got too much outstanding," they said. "We want this note and that one too." But my friend didn't have the cash to cover those notes. He trusted his "system" to keep him safe and forgot his mortgages made him a servant. He forgot that his signature gave the bank authority to call the shots in his relationship with them. They did, and it went very badly for him.

But the good news is that by diligently setting priorities for our finances and using wisdom in our financial dealings, we never have to go without. At the end of the day, we can still eat, sleep comfortably, and play. We can still enjoy nice things and take our families on vacation; we just do those things without neglecting our other responsibilities.

Every dollar spent can be classified as going toward assets, liabilities, or necessities. Now some of these things are circumstantial; they can vary depending on where you live and what you do. Others may cross categories, but generally, an asset is something that makes money. A liability takes money. And a necessity is essential to your life.

Necessities would include food, shelter, transportation, and clothing. You must have these things to survive and keep a job. Of all the categories, this one is the most variable. Depending on where you live, you may be able to fulfill all your transportation needs through public transit instead of having a personal vehicle. Depending on your profession, you might require a special wardrobe that can't be used in other circumstances. That makes this part of your budget higher than average. Even the geographical differences, which cause fuel and food prices and options to vary, affect this category. So instead of getting hung up on numbers, just understand that anything beyond what is necessary would be classified as a liability. For example, I knew a guy who often took his large family out to eat. They regularly went to steak houses for dinner. He came to me one day and said, "I'm having trouble paying my rent. What should I do?" I thought, *Stop eating at steak houses!* Not that restaurants are a bad place to go, but if you're struggling to pay your bills, there's a difference between necessary food and restaurant-quality steak! His necessity had become a liability.

A liability is something you spend money on that doesn't provide anything in return. It could take your money up front or it could take it monthly, but liabilities only take (lose value). For example, a car can be a liability. While it may be necessary for your life, it loses value over time. Not only do all cars require insurance and maintenance, but regular gas and occasional repairs will also dent your wallet. And if you buy the car on credit, you'll have monthly payments to make (plus interest). I had a friend who saved up $7,000 for a car, but instead of paying cash for a good used vehicle, he got a new $35,000 truck and used his $7,000 as a down payment. He bought one hunk of a liability!

Consumer debt is also a liability. As is any type of membership or communications contract. Not that these are bad things, but financially, they are considered liabilities because they take money from your hand.

An asset would be something you buy that gives you a return. It adds money to your account. It could be something you buy and sell at a profit. It could be something that creates dividends or a business that nets profits. Stocks, bonds, and portfolio investments would all be considered assets. A rental property with a positive cash flow is also an asset. Publication royalties, mineral rights, or anything else that produces income is an asset.

Proverbs talks about a successful woman of noble character who used her income to buy assets and increase her household. It says she,

> Willingly works with her hands...provides food for her household...She considers a field and buys it; from her profits she plants a vineyard...she extends her hand to the poor, yes she reaches out her hands to the needy. She is not afraid of snow for her household, for all her household is clothed with scarlet...She makes linen garments and sells them...she shall rejoice in time to come...She watches over the ways of her household and does not eat the bread of idleness. Her children arise and call her blessed; her husband also, and he praises her.
>
> Proverbs 31:13-28

Why should you know the difference between assets and liabilities? Because that's what creates cash flow. Basically, cash flow is your income (assets) minus your expenses or liabilities. An important building block of financial freedom is the creation of a positive cash flow. You want to spend less than you make. If you can do that, then no matter how much (or how little) you make, you will always prosper. You will always have enough to support your family and enough to give. Unfortunately, nearly half of America's population lives above their means. They spend more money than they make. Those habits spell disaster. One month of living on credit (generating a negative cash flow), creates compounding financial trouble. Next month, not only do they have to pay off what they overspent the month before, but they have to pay interest on it, on top of all their normal expenses.

Using this basic financial statement, you can take your financial pulse and start viewing your finances soberly. If you discover your cash flow is out of control, take these steps:

- Do what you can to eliminate or reduce expenses.

- Look for ways to boost income.

- Temporarily use your discretionary cash to pay off debt.

That might mean selling the car you're making payments on and buying a used vehicle you can pay cash for. It could mean taking a look at your phone or insurance bill and cutting out non-essential products. Perhaps you need to cancel your cable or entertainment subscriptions and sell some of the extra "stuff" accumulating in your house. Or you may even want to get a part-time job to boost your income.

Do whatever you can to balance your cash flow. One of the best things I did when I owned a car lot was to close down my physical location. That may sound counter-productive for a car dealer, but it took a ton of money just to open my doors every day. Not only did I have to buy merchandise, but I also had to pay for staff, rent, utilities, and detailing. If I didn't sell any cars one day, the next day I had to sell twice as many to cover my expenses. If nothing sold the second day, I'd have to sell three times as many on the weekends—all while my stock devalued on the lot. It was scary. One of the best things I did was shift my business to online-only sales. When I did, my overhead tumbled and so did my stress level. I only had to sell 20 percent of my original quota to make the bills and provide for my family!

PERSONAL FINANCIAL STATEMENT
[Name]
[Date]

Assets	Amount in Dollars
Cash - checking accounts	$
Cash - savings accounts	
Certificates of deposit	
Securities - stocks / bonds / mutual funds	
Notes & contracts receivable	
Life insurance *(cash surrender value)*	
Personal property *(autos, jewelry, etc.)*	
Retirement Funds *(IRAs, 401k)*	
Real estate *(market value)*	
Other assets *(specify)*	
Other assets *(specify)*	
Total Assets	$

Liabilities	Amount in Dollars
Current Debt *(Credit cards, Accounts)*	
Notes payable *(describe below)*	
Taxes payable	
Real estate mortgages *(describe)*	
Other liabilities *(specify)*	
Other liabilities *(specify)*	
Total Liabilities	$
Net Worth	$

This simple step helped me create a positive cash flow. Soon, I had money in my hands that wasn't tied to a bill, so I began considering what to do with it. Instead of buying liabilities (the stuff that took money from my hand), I began to buy assets. I began investing in things that produced for me, and life started getting easier. I began to see God's promise to bless my storehouse come to pass (Deuteronomy 28:8).

The amazing thing is, just like over-spending (living above your means) creates an income gap that grows exponentially larger if not corrected, under-spending (living below your means) does too. With diligence and planning, the extra cash in your pocket can become a money-making asset that increases your income. Then, instead of buying liabilities with your extra, you can purchase assets that will increase you even more. That's how the rich get richer and are eventually able to live off their passive income alone (income they don't work for). Maybe your first step towards asset-purchasing means you create a savings account as protection from life's storms. Maybe you purchase a mutual fund or buy something you can turn around and sell at a profit. Whatever it is, think long-term. Think like an investor instead of a consumer.

What do I want my finances to look like next year?

How do I want my family to be living in five years?

What will I be able to do, when I'm debt-free?

How can I use this money wisely and steward what God has given me?

Watch as your income gap expands!

Chapter Six

The Waste-Not-Want-Not Gospel

I magine what life would look like if you had no debt. What if you had no car payments, no credit card payments, no personal loan payments, no second mortgage payments, or any other debt repayments? What if none of your money was being wasted on interest? How much money would you have? How would you live? What would you do with your extra income? Have you ever allowed yourself to dream like that? You should, because that's how God dreams for you. And that is the type of living He made you for!

> For I know the thoughts that I think toward you, says the LORD, thoughts of peace and not of evil, to give you a future and a hope.
>
> Jeremiah 29:11

> Beloved, I pray that you may prosper in all things and be in health, just as your soul prospers.
>
> 3 John 2

Another aspect of stewardship is debt management. A lot of people don't like to talk about debt, but nearly all of us have experienced it to some degree. Contrary to popular Christian culture, debt is not sin. If debt were sin, God would never have said in Deuteronomy 15:6, "You shall lend to many nations but you shall not borrow." He would never have sanctioned putting someone else into sin by making them a borrower. But debt, if not managed properly, can cause great stress and even heartache in our lives. As mentioned before, debt creates a master-servant relationship (Proverbs 22:7), even amongst family and friends. I personally never borrow from or lend to family and friends. My relationship with them is too valuable!

There are two main types of debt: consumer debt and investment or business debt. Consumer debt would be the debt we carry on liabilities or things that lose value over time. Business or investment debt would be debt on assets or things that increase their value over time. Some people call business debt "good debt" because, if structured correctly, someone else pays the principal and interest on it while the asset increases in value. I don't really like assigning "good" and "bad" labels to debt. I believe God's ideal is for us to be 100 percent debt free.

When God gave Moses the law, He included instructions for how to deal with debt. He listed guidelines for interest rates, timelines for repayment, and even requirements for debt forgiveness that He expected the Israelites to obey (Leviticus 25:37, Exodus 22, Deuteronomy 15). He said;

And the LORD will make you the head and not the tail; you shall be above only, and not be beneath, if you heed the commandments of the LORD your God, which I command you today, and are careful to observe them.

Deuteronomy 28:13

These things God promises can only happen if we eliminate our consumer debt as the first step to becoming debt-free. One of the most dangerous forms of consumer debt is credit card debt. On average, people using credit cards to manage negative cash flow will end up paying twice for every item they put on it due to high interest rates. And most people who use credit cards end up spending 12 percent more than those using cash, even at McDonalds!

Something happens when you physically see money exchange hands. It's easier to swallow the prices of a supersized meal when you don't watch the extra three to five dollars leaving your pocket. Using cash creates emotional pain. It unconsciously adds a level of accountability to your spending habits. With cash, you can only spend what you have.

But I have to have a credit score! Why? So you can get more debt? All a credit score does is tell a bank whether or not you have a habit of paying your bills. It gives them an idea of your debt-to-income ratio and tells them if you're a safe person to lend to. *But I can't get a loan without a credit score!* I did.

The last house I bought, I bought without any credit history—no credit cards, no car loans, nothing. I put 20 percent down and got a great fixed rate. How? I proved I was responsible with my finances. The local bank I worked with asked to see my checking account statements and a personal financial statement that compared my debt and income. I also got a letter of recommendation from my previous landlord to detail how I'd paid my rent. The bank didn't have any trouble underwriting me.

Did you know that living on credit has not always been a way of life? The first credit card wasn't issued until 1960. Before that, most people paid for their daily necessities with cash. If they wanted to purchase a larger-ticketed item, they saved until they had enough cash to buy it.

In most cases, credit is the opposite of stewardship, It's wasteful. Our God is a god of supernatural abundance, a God of multiplication, but He's not a god of waste. God is a good steward. When Jesus fed the 5,000 with only five loaves of bread and two small fish, there was an abundance of food for everyone. After everyone had eaten their fill, Jesus told the disciples to pick up all the leftovers. He didn't want any of it going to waste. They picked up 12 baskets full (Matthew 14:13-21)!

I bought a used travel trailer a while back and was fascinated when I found the original credit agreement. The people I bought it from had purchased the trailer on credit in 1998 for $12,000. Somehow, they were convinced to purchase this luxury item on credit for "only $136 a month" for the next 144 months. (For all you math whizzes, that meant the term of their contract was 12 years!) The original owners used the trailer twice a year, and ten years later, sold it to me for $2,500. But here's the kicker. After ten years of faithfully making their monthly payments, they paid $18,070 for that trailer and still hadn't paid it off when they sold it to me. When I bought the trailer, they still owed $3,416 on it.

I offered $2,500 cash for their ten-year-old trailer, and they jumped at the chance to get rid of it, even though they still had to come up with an additional $1000 to finishing paying it off. I bet when they bought the trailer, all they saw as the easy monthly payments. They didn't consider how much they'd actually be paying for it. The couple ended up paying over $21,000 for their trailer—nearly double its original price! Would that have happened if they used cash? I doubt it.

I remember depositing some cash in my bank account recently. I only put in about half of what I was carrying and the teller said, "It's not safe to carry cash around like that. Don't you want to deposit the rest?"

"No," I responded, "it's perfectly safe to carry cash."

"You might get robbed," he said.

"But if I get robbed," I answered, "all I can lose is what I've got. If I had a credit card, I could go down to that furniture or appliance store and get 'robbed' of what I haven't got. Then I'd be paying for it for three to five years!"

But my credit card has awesome rewards, people often say. I'm not suggesting they don't, but how much more do you spend to qualify for those rewards? Let me just say, the credit card company isn't losing money offering a card to you! I personally don't own credit cards, nor will I. I'm not condemning anyone for using credit, but no one ever said, "My credit card rewards prospered me. That's what got me ahead." However, I have heard people say, "Credit card debt is what pulled me down. It was so easy to get in over my head." Again, I'm not negating their convenience, but I've seen too many negative consequences to personally get involved with consumer credit.

A good alternative to buying with credit (if you don't want to carry cash) is a debit card. I use debit cards all the time. With a debit card, you still get the convenience of carrying plastic (you can easily rent vehicles and hotel rooms or shop online), but you have the safety net of only being able to spend what you have. The average American household has upwards of $15,000 in credit card debt—and that doesn't include other small loans like cars, furniture, or department store lines of credit.

If you're sinking in debt, stop the cycle of overspending and take action to free yourself. Make a plan, and write it down, just like you wrote out your prosperity goals in a previous chapter (Habakkuk 2:2). Figure out exactly how much consumer debt you have. List all your credit cards, store cards, and small loans (don't include your business debt or home mortgages here) in order from smallest balance to greatest. Include each line of credit's minimum payment amount on your plan.

Now take a deep breath and look at your obligations. Without ignoring any of them (in other words, keep making your minimum payments), start putting all your extra income towards paying off the smallest debt on your list. When that debt is cleared, cancel the card and roll the payments you were making on it to the next largest debt. Keep eliminating balances one by one using this debt snowball.

Even though it seems to start too small to make a lasting impact, the longer you use the debt snowball, the larger its effect will become. If you are diligent and cut out all nonessential spending during this process, soon all your debt will be swallowed up and you will experience financial freedom! Some short term sacrifices and hard work today literally have the potential to change the rest of your life.

"But I can barely make my minimum payments," you say. "How am I going to put more money towards debt to pay it off?" Look for something you can sell. Do you have things in your house you don't need or can live without? If you haven't used something for a year and it has no sentimental value, sell it. Have a garage sale. Utilize Craigslist or eBay and turn that stuff into cash.

But it's no longer worth what I paid for it. It's not worth anything just sitting there either. So sell it, and put that cash towards your first debt. Once the first debt is paid off, you'll at least have its minimum payment to add to the next debt on the list.

There is hope. Not only is God your source, but He is also your help (Psalm 33:20, 46:10). You'll be amazed to discover the supernatural help you get when you put your hands to work tackling debt. *You just don't understand. My debt is overwhelming.* Isn't our God a god of impossible things? He can make a way where there seems to be no way (2 Samuel 22:33, Isaiah 43:16, and 1 Corinthians 10:13). Trust Him. Let Him show Himself strong on your behalf, but give Him something to work with (2 Chronicles 16:9)! Remember, we appropriate His grace with active faith.

Stewardship is active faith. It's a part of who God is, and subsequently, part of who we are in Christ. One time when a fish accidently swallowed a coin in the sea, Jesus told Peter to catch the fish, take the coin out of its mouth, and pay their taxes (Matthew 17:27). Another time, a man approached Elijah about his axe lost at the bottom of the river. God told Elijah how to keep the axe head from being wasted. Elijah threw a stick in the water, and the axe head floated to the top (2 Kings 6:1-7). Even in creation, God made everything with purpose and in order. He didn't make plants before there was a sun to feed them. He didn't make birds until there was a place to put them. And He didn't make man until there was something for him to do (Genesis 1-2). God stewards everything. He uses resources wisely.

Many Christians think that since God is a god of supernatural provision, it doesn't matter how they use their resources. But that's not true. It does matter. Ultimately, the heart attitudes we have about possessions and the way we use money now will only be magnified when we have more. According to scripture, if we can't properly steward what we have now, we won't properly steward anything else we might be given (Luke 16:12).

For to everyone who has, more will be given, and he will have abundance; but from him who does not have, even what he has will be taken away.

Matthew 25:29

This is a waste-not-want-not gospel!

Part Three

Oil Jars

I have been young, and now am old; Yet I have not seen the righteous forsaken, Nor his descendants begging bread.

Psalm 35:27

Chapter Seven

In Position

There is nothing we can do to make God bless us. God made the decision to do that a long time ago and provided for us in Christ. He already blessed us. He already made us prosperous. Ultimately, everything we "do" (our work, our stewardship, our giving) is a fruit of that prosperity. God has positioned us for prosperity. He has positioned us for success. But how many of us have moved away from God's positioning?

It's easy to do. It's easy to get distracted by what is urgent and forget about what is necessary. Martha did.

> Now it happened as they went that He entered a certain village; and a certain woman named Martha welcomed Him into her house. And she had a sister called Mary, who also sat at Jesus' feet and heard His word. But Martha was distracted with much serving, and she approached Him and said, "Lord, do You not care that my sister has left me to serve alone? Therefore tell her to help me." And Jesus answered and said to her, "Martha, Martha, you are worried and troubled about many things.

But one thing is needed, and Mary has chosen that good part, which will not be taken away from her."

Luke 10:38-41

If you remember your Bible trivia, Mary and Martha were the sisters of Lazarus. Over the years, they developed a relationship with the Lord and spent a considerable amount of time with Him (Luke 10:38, John 11:5, Matthew 26:6-7). But on this particular day, Martha got distracted.

Now let me just point out that Mary was not the slacker everyone seems to think she was. In verse 40, Martha came to Jesus complaining that Mary "left her to serve alone." Mary had been helping her sister prepare, but she stopped to listen to Jesus. Let me also say that people's perception of Martha is wrong as well. She was not a workaholic. Notice verse 39 says, "Martha had a sister called Mary who also sat at Jesus' feet." Apparently, both women began their visits at the Lord's feet. But Martha got distracted with the need to serve.

I would say, on this particular day, the women knew Jesus was coming to their house. (Chances are He had stayed there before.) They both probably spent the morning preparing. I'm certain, like most women, they had to ensure the house was clean, the food prepped, and no laundry was left hanging on the line. They probably traveled back and forth to the well many times to get enough water for their tasks. Maybe they even prepared a special dessert for their company. When Jesus finally arrived, both women were ready for a break and gratefully sat at His feet to enjoy their visit.

However, as more and more people heard Jesus was in town and staying at Lazarus' home, the crowd gathering in Martha's parlor increased. Soon, Martha began counting heads. *I don't have enough food for all these people*, she thought. *What am I going to do?* So she got up. She left Jesus' feet and began scrounging around her kitchen. *I've got flour, oil, and figs*, she may have thought. *But I'm out of eggs. Perhaps I can borrow some from my neighbor.* The longer she remained in the kitchen, the more distracted she got. *I don't have enough meat. I need more wine. I don't have enough plates!*

Eventually, she became so stressed that she approached Jesus and said, "Lord, do You not care that my sister has left me to serve alone?" What she was really saying was, "Can't You see I'm trying to make this impromptu meeting successful?" Jesus replied, "Martha, you're worried. Only one thing is needed and Mary has chosen it. I'll not take it from her."

Martha didn't need to take the burden of success upon herself; she didn't need to leave her position. There was nothing she could do to physically provide for all those people, but she was in relationship with Jesus, and He could do something. (Remember this was the guy who had just fed 5,000 people with a little boy's lunch!) Unfortunately, when Martha took herself out of position, she also stopped herself from receiving. She stopped hearing the Word and experiencing its benefits and instead became anxious. Who knows? If she had stayed in position, maybe there would have been another miracle recorded that day!

If we're not careful, we can do the same thing. We can try to make God's promises happen in our own strength. *Should I ask for more hours? Will I get that promotion? Did I save enough last month? Can I invest more? Should I give here or try this?* The problem is all our doing gets us so busy with life and caught up in its cares that we forget relationship—relationship with God, with His Word, and with our families. Doing so removes us from correct positioning.

Prosperity is a fruit (a byproduct) of our relationship with Christ. God made us prosperous in Christ Jesus.

> For you know the grace of our Lord Jesus Christ, that though He was rich, yet for your sakes He became poor, that you through His poverty might become rich.
>
> 2 Corinthians 8:9

> I know your affliction and distress and pressing trouble and your poverty—but you are rich!
>
> Revelation 2:9 AMP

Regardless of our circumstances, this is who we are. If we maintain our position, the fruit of who we are will produce itself in our lives naturally.

So how do we remain in a position to receive from God? We must first remember that our position derives from relationship. Without Christ, none of the benefits of our salvation are possible (2 Peter 1:3, Romans 5:10-11). Second, remember that we receive from God by grace (His undeserved, good intentions toward us) through faith (Ephesians 2:8 and Romans 5:2). And lastly, our faith must be active. We must do something with what we profess to believe (James 2:14-26).

I remember when Carlie and I first started Bible school; we left our business to move to another part of the country. Because of our class schedules, we couldn't work regular 9:00 to 5:00 jobs, but we knew God was our provision.

At times, it felt like things couldn't get any tighter. Yet every time, we'd watch God faithfully provide for our kids' needs and our tuition payments. One particular time, Carlie and I were praying and believing God for extra finances. We both felt the Lord tell us, "The provision is in your house." Neither of us could figure out what that meant, but we held onto it in faith.

Then one day, my wife was cleaning. As she vacuumed, she continued to thank God that the provision we were believing for was already in our house. Suddenly, she noticed the corner of an envelope sticking out of a gap between our wall and baseboards. In the envelope was a check for several thousand dollars dated four months earlier! Apparently, the mailman got a little carried away with his delivery that day, and one of our letters got separated from the rest. (In England, most houses have letterboxes in their front doors so all the mail is delivered inside the house.)

A few days later, I was going through my filing cabinet and found a certificate for a personalized license plate I owned. (In England, personalized plates are privately owned. You can buy and sell them like any other personal property.) I had taken the plate off my car years ago, but still had the title for it. I decided to list it on eBay. It sold and paid an entire year's college tuition for us both!

The provision we needed was in our house. God had provided for us, we just hadn't gotten into position to see it. Those instances got me thinking. I realized God was providing for us in ways I hadn't considered, and I determined to stop limiting His provision to what I had experienced in the past (1 Corinthians 2:14). I determined to listen to His Word and act on it in faith. I determined to stay in position.

We need to learn to recognize God's provision. Some things He does are only for a season; they don't follow the patterns we've seen before, they seem bizarre or too natural. But in God's hands, they become supernatural!

We see this happening in a familiar story from 2 Kings.

A certain woman of the wives of the sons of the prophets cried out to Elisha, saying, "Your servant my husband is dead, and you know that your servant feared the LORD. And the creditor is coming to take my two sons to be his slaves." So Elisha said to her, "What shall I do for you? Tell me, what do you have in the house?" And she said, "Your maidservant has nothing in the house but a jar of oil." Then he said, "Go, borrow vessels from everywhere, from all your neighbors—empty vessels; do not gather just a few. And when you have come in, you shall shut the door behind you and your sons; then pour it into all those vessels, and set aside the full ones." So she went from him and shut the door behind her and her sons, who brought the vessels to her; and she poured it out. Now it came to pass, when the vessels were full, that she said to her son, "Bring me another vessel." And he said to her, "There is not another vessel." So the oil ceased. Then she came and told the man of God. And he said, "Go, sell the oil and pay your debt; and you and your sons live on the rest."

2 Kings 4:1-7

This widow woman found herself in great need of God's provision. Her husband who had worked for Elisha, died with outstanding debts. She had no means of paying for these debts and was fearful that the creditors would come to make her two sons slaves. She did the only thing she knew to do. She got into position and called on her relationship with Elisha.

It's interesting that the first thing Elisha asked the woman was, "What do you have in your house?" Elisha knew that the supernatural always starts with something natural. I'm sure the widow thought, *It's hopeless; I have nothing of value.* But when Elisha asked, she said, "There's a jar of oil." "Okay," Elisha said, "God can work with that."

Elisha gave her instructions to borrow empty vessels and fill them with her oil. I'm sure the woman thought, *How am I supposed to fill all those vessels? My own vessel isn't even full!* But she heard the word and acted on it in faith; she stayed in position. She began collecting vessels, and when she'd gathered all the empty vessels she could find, Elisha told her to shut the door and start pouring.

Why did Elisha tell her to shut the door? Why did Jesus shut the door when He raised the little girl from the dead in Luke 8:49-56? Why did He tell the disciples to pray with their doors shut in Matthew 6:6? I believe shutting the door is a symbolic way for us to get rid of unbelief. When you believe God for something supernatural, you can't listen to everyone else's opinions or experiences and still believe. You have to make a conscious effort to "shut the door" on unbelief, even in your own mind. Romans says Abraham didn't consider the reasons God's promises wouldn't work in his life. He simply chose to believe (Romans 4:19).

When the widow woman followed the man of God's instructions, she received her miracle. She didn't take away from his instructions. She didn't add to them. She simply obeyed, and it came to pass when the vessels were full, the oil stopped. Notice how her faith determined the size of her harvest. Notice how the oil ceased as soon as she had no place else to put it. I believe if she'd had 20 more jars, the oil would have kept multiplying, but because God is a god of stewardship, none of the oil was wasted or spilled out on the ground.

We've been given instructions, too. They're in the Word of God. If, like the widow, we obey those instructions, we will see the supernatural overflow of God's provision in our lives. But the overflow can only flow where the overflow can flow. If there's nowhere for God's supernatural flow to go or no way to use it, it cannot flow in our lives (and I'm not just talking about finances).

Part of being in position is having a place for the supernatural abundance of God to go. What would you do with an extra $1,000 this month? An extra $5,000? Do you have another jar? Do you have a plan (2 Corinthians 9:7)? Who can you give to? Where can you pay down debt? What can you invest in? Asking God to give you abundance when you don't have a place for it to go is like asking Him to pour oil on the floor. He can't do that. It's wasteful; it goes against His nature.

We have to position ourselves to receive the blessings of God. For example, we all have favor. Psalms says we are surrounded with God's favor like a shield (Psalm 5:12), but we can choose not to walk in it. People say things like, "I've got favor, I'm going to a job interview, and I'm going to get that job because I have favor." Then they turn up late and unshaven in a pair of dirty jeans. They're not prepared. They don't come with an understanding of what the job entails. They're arrogant and rude, and then wonder why they didn't get the job. Wasn't the favor of God with them? Sure. Were they walking in it? Was it evident in their behavior? No, it wasn't; they didn't position themselves correctly. In Genesis, when Joseph was promoted from imprisoned slave to second-in-command, he shaved and changed his clothes before appearing before Pharaoh (Genesis 41:14). Joseph positioned himself for favor and received the blessing of God.

Let's get ourselves into position!

Chapter Eight

Don't Eat Your Seed

Prosperity, true biblical prosperity, is having balance in all areas of our lives. It includes spiritual well-being, emotional peace, physical health, relationships, and finances (3 John 2). Financially, it combines the principals of work, savings, and giving. If we aren't able to give, then we're not on God's track to true prosperity.

In 2 Corinthians, Paul said, "Let each one give as he purposes in his heart, not grudgingly or of necessity; for God loves a cheerful giver" (2 Corinthians 9:7). According to this verse, we need to give with purpose. We can't use a shotgun approach to giving. If we don't make provision for giving, we either won't have money to give or we'll give grudgingly. We must plan to give.

I hate going to supermarkets and being hit up for money. "Would you like to give a dollar to this charity? Can we add five dollars to your total and feed a child in war-torn Africa?" Even in Christian bookstores you'll hear, "Would you donate two dollars to give a Bible to someone without?" It makes me feel guilty, especially if other people are around. I might have given

50,000 dollars that year, but those questions make me feel guilty for not giving two dollars more. We should never give like that. That type of compulsory giving doesn't bless God. (And many times, the charities that are collecting money like that only use a small percentage of your donation on their advertised need. To see how your favorite charity ranks, visit charitynavigator.org.)

Never feel pressured or manipulated into giving. Paul says giving should be done "cheerfully, not grudgingly or of necessity." When you give, know where your money is going. Make sure you're giving into good ground, because money is like seed. If used properly, it multiplies and produces a harvest.

> He who sows sparingly will also reap sparingly, and he who sows bountifully will also reap bountifully.
>
> 2 Corinthians 9:6

So what constitutes a bountiful gift? That depends. One day at the temple, Jesus sat opposite of the treasury and saw people giving. He saw the wealthy putting in their large gifts and the poor putting in their smaller ones. A widowed woman approached the bucket and put in two mites. When Jesus saw her gift, He called his disciples over and said she had given more than anyone (Mark 12:41-44). What do you suppose triggered that response in Jesus? Hers surely wasn't the greatest gift, and she likely wasn't the only poor person to give either. I believe it was her attitude. She sowed willingly and cheerfully.

When we sow, we give God permission to work in our finances. When a farmer sows a field, what does he produce? A harvest. Some of that harvest he sells, some he saves as seed for next year, and some he eats. But all of it starts as seed. When we purpose in our hearts to sow, we become like a farmer and God gives us seed. Some of that seed is to be used to meet our needs (eating and bill paying). And some of it is to be sown (given). Just like the farmer, the seed we sow can multiply and produce a harvest for us.

> Now may He who supplies seed to the sower, and bread for food, supply and multiply the seed you have sown and increase the fruits of your righteousness, while you are enriched in everything for all liberality, which causes thanksgiving through us to God.
>
> 2 Corinthians 9:10-11

In Mark, when Jesus saw the poor woman giving her two mites, He called her gift generous even though it was small. Jesus didn't try to stop her from giving. He didn't go to the moneybox, pull out her offering, and return it to her saying, "Keep this. You need it to live; you can't afford to give." He knew she was sowing seed. The woman didn't need her seed returned. She needed a harvest. Jesus saw that and refused to reject her seed and uproot her harvest. (When I get to heaven, I'm going to look for that woman. I'm going to walk around with a sign like one of those limo drivers at the airport that says: "Widow woman who gave the two mites!" I want to find out what happened with her seed! I know she was supernaturally blessed because of her bountiful sowing.)

My point is if we don't have enough money to meet our needs, we may not be looking at the end result of God's provision, we may be looking at seed. There have been times in my life when all I had in my hand was seed. When we purchased our home, for instance, I asked the Lord, "How are we going to do this? This is bigger than me." His answer surprised me. He said, "Pay this for that person," and it was a big bill He was wanting me to pay! "I can do that Lord, but it will use up all we've saved for our down payment." He replied, "You don't have enough to buy a house anyway. Sow it, and trust Me for your harvest." So we did. Now we live in a house that not only meets our needs but is also a blessing to us. It was a supernatural deal, and it's still appreciating in value each month!

Even when Jesus fed the 5,000 with a little boy's lunch, the boy was sowing seed. He gave his five rolls and two fish to Jesus, not expecting to feed the multitude. But Jesus blessed it, broke it, and the little boy watched it multiply in the disciples' hands. After everyone had their fill at the original all-you-can-eat buffet, the disciples picked up 12 baskets of leftovers (one for each of them). What a harvest (Luke 9:10-17)!

This is a great story, but I wonder what would have happened if the disciples had eaten the bread instead of sown it? It was evening, they had spent all day listening to Jesus, they must have been hungry, too. I'm sure even Jesus was hungry. What would have happened if they had eaten the boy's lunch? They would have eaten the seed. There would have been no harvest.

Don't Eat Your Seed

Do we ever eat our seed? Second Corinthians says God gives seed to the sower and bread for food, but which comes first? In a farmer's life, seed comes first. Without seed, there is no harvest from which he can sell, eat, and sow again. It's the same for us. If we eat all the seed God gives us, we'll short circuit the system. We won't have enough to sow and therefore, won't see a harvest. Remember, only the seed sown can be multiplied.

God gives us seed. His Word shows us the principles we need to follow to ensure that seed multiplies and produces a harvest for us. Sometimes though, we eat our seed. We consume it ourselves or sow it along the path (Matthew 13:1-9). Then we feel discouraged looking for a nonexistent harvest. We need to ask the Lord, "What part of this provision is seed? What is for my daily food?" We need to rely on our relationship with Him and learn to follow His instructions to the letter.

I was at a mission's banquet one winter; they filled the hall with tables and fancy dishes (servers dressed in black and white) and delicious smelling food. Unfortunately, a snowstorm hit that afternoon, and no one came. It was so sad. (They sat all of us who came at one round table.) I was thinking, *What a shame*, but I got up and took up the offering anyway, as I had been asked to. Then the missionary got up and spoke.

It was a typical "this is what we're doing" presentation, but then he said something that stuck with me. He said Oral Roberts told him, "When you pray in the Holy Spirit, usually the first thing that comes to mind is from God. Then we try to talk ourselves out of it." *That's an interesting concept*, I thought. *I have never heard it said like that before.*

When the evening came to a close, I left the church and began praying in the Holy Spirit. *BAM!* Clear as day, a thought popped into my mind, *That money in the bank that you saved for the down payment, give it to the missionary.* "Whoa," I said to myself. "I didn't hear that. That thought must have come from my flesh or the devil!" I'm just being honest. My selfish, self-seeking flesh was getting seriously concerned!

I got in my truck and phoned my wife in tears. She said, "You don't even know this missionary. This sounds crazy."

"It's God, Carlie. I'm telling you, it's God."

"If you think it's God," she said, "then do it."

So the next day (I had to get myself together first), I called the missionary and asked to meet with him. When we got together, I handed him a cashier's check. It was the biggest one-time offering I'd ever given; one of the largest of my faith checks. (Years before I had written out faith checks of different amounts that I believed God I'd be able to give one day. I didn't date them. I didn't address them. I never gave them away. They stayed locked in my safe. But I wanted to see myself as a giver, so I wrote them out, just for practice. They were my giving goals.)

This missionary broke down in tears when he looked at my check. He was trying to build a Bible school in Yangon, Myanmar, and that offering covered the cost. A while later, he sent us a newsletter. They built the school, graduated their first class of 24 missionaries and pastors, and sent them all around the world! Who knows what that seed is going to look like in a few more years!

You know, it felt good to give him that gift, even though my flesh struggled with it. I remember driving in my truck the next day thanking God for the opportunity to give when I heard Him clearly say, "No, Ashley. Thank you." Well, that got me. I had to pull over. *God, the Creator of the universe is thanking me! Who am I?* I felt Him say, "Some people don't even have it on their radar to give that amount of money. You weren't the first person I asked to give that amount. The others couldn't hear Me; giving like that wasn't even on their radar." I realized that unless you're prepared to give, you won't. Since I already prepared my heart to (eventually) give that amount of money, when God said it, I could hear and obey.

Of course, there is wisdom to consider in this. God never asks us to give away our bread. He supplies both "seed for the sower and bread for food" (2 Corinthians 9:10). But He promises that when you give of your seed generously, you're going to reap generously (2 Corinthians 9:6). "I don't have enough to be a generous giver," you say. Remember the widow with her two mites. God says everyone can be a generous giver. The amount doesn't matter; it's about your attitude.

Giving is the highest use of your money. In 1 Kings, Elijah met a widow woman picking up sticks. There was a drought in the land, and she was collecting fuel to make the last of her food for supper before laying down to die (1 Kings 17:12). Elijah asked the woman for a drink of water (something that was also in very short supply) and a meal. But she didn't have a meal to give. "All I have is a handful of flour in a bin and a little oil in a jar," she said. "That's only enough to make something small for myself and my son before we die." Elijah knew the best use of her resources was in the kingdom of God. "Make your cake," he said, "but give it to me first." She did, and God supplied for her needs throughout the entire drought. She and her son never went hungry (1 Kings 17:8-13).

> I have been young, and now am old; yet I have not seen the righteous forsaken, nor his descendants begging bread.
>
> Psalm 37:25

The Kingdom of God is a safe investment. A wise man gives what he cannot keep in order to gain what he cannot lose. Jesus said;

> Assuredly, I say to you, there is no one who has left house or brothers or sisters or father or mother or wife or children or lands, for My sake and the gospel's, who shall not receive a hundredfold now in this time—houses and brothers and sisters and mothers and children and lands, with persecutions—and in the age to come, eternal life.
>
> Mark 10:29-30 (emphasis added)

You cannot keep your possessions. It doesn't matter if you've got gold or diamonds; it doesn't matter if you build your house out of steel and bricks. You cannot keep anything in this life. But everything you give away, you get to keep.

> For whoever desires to save his life will lose it, but whoever loses his life for My sake and the gospel's will save it. For what will it profit a man if he gains the whole world, and loses his own soul?
>
> Mark 8:35-36

> Do not lay up for yourselves treasures on earth, where moth and rust destroy and where thieves break in and steal; but lay up for yourselves treasures in heaven, where neither moth nor rust destroys and where thieves do not break in and steal.
>
> Matthew 6:19-20

That's the principle behind giving. When you give and see a soul come into the kingdom or see someone touched by the love of God, you touch God's heart. You touch eternity. It's all about people. And God will not be out-given! If you get addicted to giving, God will support your habit!

> Give, and it will be given to you: good measure, pressed down, shaken together, and running over will be put into your bosom. For with the same measure that you use, it will be measured back to you.
>
> Luke 6:38

Chapter Nine

The Violence of Giving

God is a giver; He's not a taker. Giving is part of His nature. It's who He is and how He operates. John 3:16 says He "so loved the world that He gave." And He didn't give a little; God gave the best He had. He gave Jesus. God doesn't need your money. There's not a financial crisis in heaven. Psalms says, "The earth is the LORD's, and all its fullness, the world and those who dwell therein" (Psalm 24:1). In another place it says, "For the beast of the forest is Mine, and the cattle on a thousand hills" (Psalm 50:10). God owns everything. He does not need your money. So why does God ask us to give? Because He wants our heart (Matthew 6:19-21), and somehow finances trigger a heart response.

> No servant can serve two masters; for either he will hate the one and love the other, or else he will be loyal to one and despise the other. You cannot serve both God and mammon [money].
>
> Luke 16:13 (brackets added)

The Bible details three different kinds of giving. The first is tithing. I know there's a huge debate in the church about tithing, but I personally believe we should tithe. Many people argue that tithing is part of the law and was therefore canceled with Jesus' sacrifice. But tithing happened before the law. In Genesis, Abraham returned from war and gave a tenth of all the spoils (tithing) to Melchizedek, the king of Salem (Genesis 14:18-20).

Tithing is a principle not a law. A principle is something that is right to do in every situation. A law is based on a cause-and-effect relationship. Think of it this way: murder was before the law (Cain killed Abel in Genesis 4); murder became part of the law when God added a consequence to it (Exodus 20:13, Numbers 35); and murder is after the law (just look at our prisons). Murder is wrong; it's always been wrong. It will always be wrong, regardless of whether or not there is a consequence for it. Tithing, too, was before the law (Abraham tithed to Melchizedek). Tithing became part of the law when God added a consequence for not tithing (Malachi 3:8-9). And tithing is after the law. The only difference is that since Jesus fulfilled the law, the consequence for not tithing is removed. But the principle of tithing—the spirit behind it—remains.

> Honor the LORD with your possessions, and with the firstfruits of all your increase.
>
> Proverbs 3:9

> Bring all the tithes into the storehouse, that there may be food in My house, and try Me now in this," says the LORD of hosts, "If I will not open for you the windows

of heaven and pour out for you such blessing that there will not be room enough to receive it.

Malachi 3:10

Tithing is ultimately about putting God first. In Genesis 28, Jacob made a vow to God. He said, "of all that You give me, I will surely give a tenth" (Genesis 28:22). Again, this was before the law, so we know Jacob wasn't coerced into giving. He wasn't fearful of the consequences of not giving. Jacob's tithe was a way of honoring God. When you tithe, you should tithe where you're being fed in support of that ministry (1 Corinthians 9:11-14). Remember that we're not tithing with an attitude of paying God His ten percent and keeping 90 percent to do whatever we want. One hundred percent of everything we have is God's. Tithing helps us remember that. It's a faith statement that says, "I know You are my provider. Everything I have is Yours. As I honor You, help me be a good steward of all You've given me." Our tithe honors God and gives Him permission to bless us.

Under the law, not tithing cursed you with lack, but Galatians 3:13 says that, "Christ has redeemed us from the curse of the law." We don't tithe today out of fear of being cursed. Jesus removed the consequences of the law. Today we tithe to allow God the opportunity to bless us with the benefits of obedience (Malachi 3:8-11).

Another type of giving listed in the Bible is offerings. Some people get confused about this, but giving offerings has nothing to do with need. In the Old Testament, offerings were given in the context of relationship (Exodus 20:24). They were a tangible representation of the Israelites' desire to communicate with God. There's a great story in 1 Kings, which illustrates this. The queen of Sheba came to visit King Solomon and introduced herself with a gift.

> When the queen of Sheba heard about the fame of Solomon and his relationship to the LORD, she came to test Solomon with hard questions…Solomon answered all her questions; nothing was too hard for the king to explain to her…She said to the king…"Praise be to the LORD your God, who has delighted in you and placed you on the throne of Israel. Because of the LORD's eternal love for Israel, he has made you king to maintain justice and righteousness." And she gave the king 120 talents of gold, large quantities of spices, and precious stones. Never again were so many spices brought in as those the queen of Sheba gave to King Solomon.
>
> 1 Kings 10:1,3,9-10

Now obviously, Solomon didn't need the queen's gift. He was the richest man to ever live on our planet. (Apparently, she was doing alright too, to afford such an extravagant gift!) The queen desired relationship with Solomon,. She wanted to talk with him, ask him questions, and perhaps even participate in the blessings and wisdom he had. The Bible says that when Solomon accepted her gift, the desires of her heart were fulfilled.

Her offering opened the door to relationship with Solomon. However, it's important to note that she came with a pure heart.

The Violence of Giving

The queen of Sheba wasn't trying to manipulate Solomon into spending time with her. She genuinely wanted to acknowledge the work she saw God performing in his life and do what she could to encourage him (1 Kings 10:6-8).

We should give our offerings to ministers and missionaries who are successfully walking in the things God has appointed for them—meeting people's spiritual and physical needs. When we do, we acknowledge and support what God is doing through them. We also enter into relationship with them and align ourselves to share in their reward (Matthew 10:41).

The third type of giving mentioned in the Bible is benevolence giving. Benevolence giving identifies needs and meets them. In Matthew, Jesus said,

> For I was hungry and you gave me something to eat, I was thirsty and you gave me something to drink, I was a stranger and you invited me in, I needed clothes and you clothed me, I was sick and you looked after me, I was in prison and you came to visit me.
>
> Matthew 25:35-36

When we give to meet someone's physical needs, we show them God's heart of compassion. We show them they are important. And when we share with others in this way, Jesus said it's like directly giving to Him.

> Whoever is kind to the poor lends to the LORD, and he will reward them for what they have done.
>
> Proverbs 19:17

Giving helps us serve God and frees us from the love of money. The love of money is a dangerous thing. It caused the rich young ruler to give up following Jesus, it drew Judas out to betray Jesus, it killed Ananias and Saphira, and it has been the downfall of many modern-day ministries (Mark 10:17-22, Matthew 26:14-16, and Acts 5:1-10).

> For the love of money is the root of all kinds of evil, for which some have strayed from the faith in their greediness, and have pierced themselves through with many sorrows.
>
> 1 Timothy 6:10

> He who loves silver will not be satisfied with silver; nor he who loves abundance, with increase. This also is vanity.
>
> Ecclesiastics 5:10

The love of money is a form of covetousness, and according to Jesus' parable of the sower, it can keep the seed of the Word from producing a harvest in our life (Mark 4:18-19). But giving helps us conquer covetousness. When we give, we take money that would otherwise be spent on ourselves and give it for the benefit of others. Giving puts action to our faith and helps us "seek first His kingdom" (Matthew 6:33).

Giving guides our hearts (Proverbs 23:19). If you don't believe me, just buy something expensive and set it down somewhere, or go on vacation and lose your wallet full of cash. You'll find your mind stayed on what was lost and whether or not it could be recovered. You won't fully enjoy anything else because your heart is tied to it.

I bought a sports car once that I shouldn't have. I was at an auction, and the sun was out in England, which very rarely happens. A convertible came through the line and I thought, *It's sunny today. I could drive home with the hood down and my hair blowing in the wind.* Even though it didn't make good business sense, I wanted that car. So I got it. (And paid way too much for it!)

But it was a beautiful car—a metallic racing green that appeared to change colors in the sun. I immediately put the top down and drove that baby home with my hair streaming out behind me. It was great. True to form however, the next day it was raining so I couldn't drive it.

When I got home, my young son greeted me at the door and said, "Hi Daddy. Washed car."

"You washed my car," I asked in disbelief.

"Washed new car," he said.

"My new car," I asked again.

"Yes."

"With what, son," I asked, hoping against hope my gut instinct was wrong.

He showed me a bucket full of dirty water and gravel. "Oh, son."

"And this Daddy," he said holding up one of those plastic ice scrapers with the little bit of sponge on one end.

"You washed the car," I asked again.

I was afraid to look, but it had to be done. All along one side of my beautiful new car were tiny scratches where he'd washed. "I got all the car, Daddy," he said proudly as we walked around to the other side.

"You did, son. You got every panel," I gasped with tears in my throat. My wife thought I was touched by my son's thoughtfulness. I had been touched—kicked—right in the heart. And before I could sell that car, I got kicked again. I had to pay for a new paint job. I didn't make a dime.

The point is, wherever you put your finances is where your heart will be. If you invest in people, your heart will be about people. If you have an expensive hobby like hunting or rebuilding classic cars, your heart will be there. Every spare moment, you'll want to do your hobby; you'll even create a plan for your money with it in mind. But if you determine to give of your wealth, you can direct your heart towards the things of God.

> Do not lay up for yourselves treasure on earth, where moth and rust destroy and where thieves break in and steal; but lay up for yourselves treasures in heaven, where neither moth nor rust destroys and where thieves do not break in and steal. For where your treasure is, there your heart will be also.
>
> Matthew 6:19-21

Not only does giving reflect what's going on in our hearts,

but when we give generously and cheerfully, we reflect God's heart (2 Corinthians 9:7). God is a generous god (Psalm 51:12). Unfortunately, many professing believers are not generous. In the name of stewardship, they are stingy. Instead of reflecting God, they reflect a self-centered and fearful spirit—the opposite of who God is—and can be downright mean when it comes to their finances.

I went to a church one time that used their volunteers to rattle cans. Seriously. They'd walk around the mall shaking a jar of coins, stopping people to ask them for money. What a terrible witness! That only perpetuates the idea that Christians don't care about others; all they want is another wallet.

Let's not give that impression to people. We may be the only reflection of God's character they see. It's amazing how people respond when you go out of your way to bless them. "Why are you giving me this," they say. "I've never known a Christian who's not after my money." Generous, no-strings-attached giving shocks people. It's abnormal. But love and generosity should be the Christian's main characteristics.

A new commandment I give to you, that you love one another; as I have loved you, that you also love one another. By this all will know that you are My disciples, if you have love for one another.

John 13:34-35

Generosity shows unbelievers God's love. Long ago, I worked for a pastor who did a great job reflecting the generosity of God.

His church had regular meals together and often held functions to reach out to their community. Whenever they gathered like this, there was always a ton of food! He told me once, "When we open our doors to the community or have meals together, we always want to make sure there's more than enough so visitors feel welcome to join us. We should never portray lack, even if we go over the top. We are reflecting God's heart; we need to be generous." Loving people is how this pastor loved God.

The amazing thing about giving to reflect God's generosity is that He'll never be out-given. Have you ever been around a group of serious givers? Giving is like a game for them. They live to see how much they can give. And they don't like being out-given; sometimes it gets violent!

I was eating out with my family one day when I saw Bobby Crow, a missionary in Mexico, across the restaurant. I decided to sneak the bill and pay for his table. Later that week at a minister's conference, we met again, and he took Carlie and I out with a group of other ministers.

"I'm paying," he said before we even left the meeting.

"We'll see, Bobby," I replied while thinking, *I'm going to get this. There's no way I'm going to let him pick up the bill.*

When we got to the restaurant, Bobby grabbed our server by the collar and pulled him close to his face. "Now listen to me, Sunshine," he said, with a hugh grin on his face. "If you give this ticket to anyone but me, I will beat you." Our server laughed but looked a little nervous, so I decided to let Bobby pay!

Another time, I was in a restaurant with my family. My parents had come to visit, and we were all stopping to eat before heading out of town for vacation. Andrew Wommack thought he saw us in the parking lot, so he came inside to chat for a few minutes. After he left, we enjoyed our dinner and sat waiting for the bill. We waited and waited. I finally asked our server, "Could I have the bill, please? We'd like to get going."

"I'm sorry," she said, "but that guy visiting you paid for it."

That's unbelievable, I thought. *He only came in to say hello. I've got to get him back!*

About a month later, after a conference, I had my chance. This time Andrew had an entire table full of staff with him. When the server came over to get our drink orders I said, "Miss, please give me the bill. Don't let anyone else pay."

"It's too late, sir. Someone's already got it."

"But we just sat down," I exclaimed. "Who paid for us?"

"That man there," she said pointing to Andrew smiling at the end of the table.

I can't let this happen again, I thought. *I'm going to have to change tactics.*

"Miss," I called again. "I have to tell you, I travel with that man at the end, and he's not a very good tipper." I watched as her eyes got big before I realized what I'd just done. (By the way, Andrew is a huge tipper, and the most generous man I know. But compared to God, he's got some room to grow!)

"If you give me the bill," I told her, "I'll guarantee a 30 percent minimum tip."

"I'll see what I can do," she told me.

After our meal, she snuck me the bill, and I paid. Then Andrew approached me, "You bear false witness over me!" he said.

"Hey," I replied, "I got the ticket!"

And remember the words of the Lord Jesus, that He said, "It is more blessed to give than to receive."

Acts 20:35

Conclusion

Imagine a tripod or a three-legged stool. They can support a lot of weight. A 300-pound linebacker can sit on a three-legged stool without a problem. Even a tripod with spindly legs can hold expensive camera equipment steady. The three principals I've shared with you in this book (work, saving, and giving) work together to form a tripod of financial prosperity. This tripod, centered in God's Word, creates a solid footing which positions you for prosperity and enables you to experience financial freedom.

Some people naturally have a good work ethic; they enjoy working and love to make money. But these people can easily fall into the trap of being workaholics and experience the heartache of broken relationships. Other people have developed a fear of poverty and save everything they make. They may boast that they still have the first dollar they ever made, but these people can fall into the trap of selfishness and self-sufficiency, which makes it difficult to trust God. Still others have an inborn desire to give; they receive immense joy from giving and are always giving to every need they come across. The only problem is they give so much, they never personally have enough and so jeopardize their other financial responsibilities like providing for their families.

In order to experience true financial freedom, we need a balance of all three of these characteristics. We need to put our hands to work.

> The LORD will open to you His good treasure, the heavens, to give the rain to your land in its season, and to bless all the work of your hand. You shall lend to many nations, but you shall not borrow.
>
> Deuteronomy 28:12

We need to save...

> The LORD will command the blessing on you in your storehouses and in all to which you set your hand, and He will bless you in the land which the LORD your God is giving you.
>
> Deuteronomy 28:8

And we need to give...

> One gives freely, yet grows all the richer; another withholds what he should give, and only suffers want.
>
> Proverbs 11:24 ESV

> And remember the words of the Lord Jesus, that He said, "It is more blessed to give than to receive."
>
> Acts 20:35

A three-fold cord like this, Ecclesiastes says, is not easily broken (Ecclesiastes 4:12)!

Author's Notes

I hope you enjoyed reading through this foundational teaching. I'd like to encourage you to take some time reading this book and studying the scriptures included. Let the Holy Spirit reveal the truth of these principals from God's Word to you, and allow that Word to renew your mind and change your opinions, if necessary. Surround yourself with believers who will encourage you through this process, and be diligent. Prosperity doesn't happen overnight, but it will "come to pass, if you diligently obey the voice of the Lord your God, to observe carefully all His commandments" (Deuteronomy 28:1). You are blessed!

I'd love to hear from you! Please share your testimonies or leave feedback about this book on my website, http://www. ashleyterradez.com/. You can also find additional resources and booking information there.

PRAYER OF SALVATION

God loves you—no matter who you are, no matter what your past. God loves you so much that He gave His one and only begotten Son for you. The Bible tells us that "…whoever believes in Him shall not perish but have eternal life" (John 3:16 NIV). Jesus laid down His life and rose again so that we could spend eternity with Him in heaven and experience His absolute best on earth. If you would like to receive Jesus into your life, say the following prayer out loud and mean it from your heart.

Heavenly Father, I come to You admitting that I am a sinner. Right now, I choose to turn away from sin, and I ask You to cleanse me of all unrighteousness. I believe that Your Son, Jesus, died on the cross to take away my sins. I also believe that He rose again from the dead so that I might be forgiven of my sins and made righteous through faith in Him. I call upon the name of Jesus Christ to be the Savior and Lord of my life. Jesus, I choose to follow You and ask that You fill me with the power of the Holy Spirit. I declare that right now I am a child of God. I am free from sin and full of the righteousness of God. I am saved in Jesus' name. Amen.

If you prayed this prayer to receive Jesus Christ as your Savior for the first time, please contact us on the Web at **www.harrisonhouse.com** to receive a free book.

Or you may write to us at
Harrison House • P.O. Box 35035 • Tulsa, Oklahoma 74153

The Harrison House Vision

Proclaiming the truth and the power

Of the Gospel of Jesus Christ

With excellence;

Challenging Christians to

Live victoriously,

Grow spiritually,

Know God intimately.